TO ERR IS HUMAN, TO FORGIVE DIVINE
NEITHER OF WHICH IS MARINE CORPS POLICY

Compiled by MSgt A. A. Bufalo USMC (Ret)

ISBN 978-0-9745793-4-4

First Printing – November 2004
Printed in the United States of America

www.AllAmericanBooks.com

To Err Is Human, To Forgive Divine

OTHER BOOKS BY ANDY BUFALO

SWIFT, SILENT & SURROUNDED
Sea Stories and Politically Incorrect Common Sense

THE OLDER WE GET, THE BETTER WE WERE
MORE Sea Stories and Politically Incorrect Common Sense
Book II

NOT AS LEAN, NOT AS MEAN, STILL A MARINE!
However, Neither is Marine Corps Policy
Even MORE Sea Stories and Politically Incorrect Common Sense
Book III

THE ONLY EASY DAY WAS YESTERDAY
Fighting the War on Terrorism

HARD CORPS
The Legends of the Marine Corps

AMBASSADORS IN BLUE
In Every Clime and Place
Marine Security Guards Protecting Our Embassies Around the World

HOLLYWOOD MARINES
Celebrities Who Served in the Corps

THE LORE OF THE CORPS
Quotations By, For & About Marines

To Err Is Human, To Forgive Divine

PREFACE

Being a Marine is a tough and often thankless task, and when the going gets rough, more times than not, it is our sense of humor that gets us through those difficult times. Marines can find humor in almost anything! And we usually we don't have to look very far.

Sometimes I think the French, and of course the Army, Navy and Air Force, were put on this earth for the sole purpose of keeping Marines amused - and they never seem to let us down.

"Old salts" will probably recognize a number of the jokes in this book - what I like to call the "oldies but goodies" – which have been passed along from one generation of Marines to the next. Some of them *still* make me laugh. But there is also a lot of new material which will surely liven up your next Mess Night.

The bottom line is, keep on laughing. It will get you through almost anything. Remember, in the Marine Corps, "the only easy day…was yesterday."

Semper Fi

To Err Is Human, To Forgive Divine

Table of Contents

To Err Is Human, To Forgive Divine

To Err Is Human, To Forgive Divine

To Err Is Human, To Forgive Divine

To Err Is Human, To Forgive Divine

INTER-SERVICE RIVALRY

"If the Army and the Navy,
Ever look on Heaven's scenes,
They will find the streets are guarded,
by United States Marines!"
- The Marines' Hymn

To Err Is Human, To Forgive Divine

IN THE BEGINNING

And on the eighth day, God created Marines...

Most Marines believe the Corps was founded at Tun Tavern on 10 November 1775, but here is what really happened:

*I*n the beginning was the word and the word was God and all else was darkness and void and without form. So God created the heavens and the earth; He created the sun and the moon and the stars, so that light might pierce the darkness. And the earth God divided between the land and the sea and the sky and He filled them with many creatures.

*A*nd the dark, salty, slimy creatures that inhabited the murky oceans God called sailors, and he dressed them accordingly. They were foul smelling and slovenly and had long hair and beards to cover their faces.

*A*nd the flighty creatures of the sky He called airmen, and these He clothed in trousers that were too short and hats too large for their heads and pockets to keep their hands warm. And because they were delicate creatures He gave them the best places to live and things for them to play with when they were not in the air.

*A*nd the creatures of the land God called soldiers. And to adorn their uniforms God gave them badges and He gave them cords and He gave them ribbons and bows... and patches... and stars. He gave them emblems... and crests... and devices that dangled and all sorts of cheap shiny things that glittered. God got carried away *bigtime.*

*O*n the seventh day God rested. And on the eighth day, at 0430, God looked down upon the earth and saw that He was not finished.

*S*o He thought about His labors, and in His infinite wisdom God knew he needed a better creature for the earth so he created a divine creature and He called it the Marine. And these Marines were magnificent. They were of the land and of the air and of the sea. And He gave them wonderful uniforms. He gave them practical fighting uniforms so they could wage war against the forces of evil anywhere. He gave them evening and dress uniforms; sharp, stylish handsome things so that they might squire the ladies on Saturday night and impress the heck outta everyone! And at the end of the eighth day, God looked down upon the earth and saw that it was good.

PETTY RIVALRY

Three college buddies were commissioned in three different branches of the armed forces - the Army, Navy, and Air Force - where they each made their careers. Although they maintained their friendship through the years, they argued long, bitterly, and inconclusively as to which service was the best. As the years wore on the three retired, grew old, and finally were called to their Heavenly rest - where they continued the dispute.

One day they encountered Saint Peter, who asked what all the fuss was about. The three officers explained their argument, and appealed to St. Peter to tell them once and for all which of their branches was the best.

Saint Peter reflected and admitted the question had never come up before. He agreed, however, to ask God and get the definitive word.

Sometime later, the officers again ran into Saint Peter and eagerly asked if he had received a reply from the Lord. Just then a snow-white dove, carrying a note in its beak, landed on Peter's shoulder. Saint Peter took the note, unfolded it, and read it to the three officers:

Gentlemen:

Your squabbling and arguing are unseemly and futile. All three of your branches were equally brave, noble, and honorable. You have all served your nation with devotion and courage. Take pride in that service, and forget your petty rivalries.

Sincerely, God
MSgt, USMC, Retired

EASY DUTY

A salty Navy Chief and a crusty Marine First Sergeant were at a bar arguing about who had the tougher career.

"I did thirty years in Recon," the Marine declared proudly, "and fought in three of my country's wars.

Fresh out of boot camp, I hit the beach at Okinawa, clawed my way up the blood-soaked sand, and eventually took out an entire enemy machine gun nest with a single grenade.

As a sergeant, I fought in Korea alongside Chesty Puller. We pushed back the enemy inch by bloody inch all the way up to the Chinese border, always under a barrage of artillery and small arms fire.

Finally, as a staff sergeant, I did three consecutive combat tours in Vietnam. We humped through the mud and razor grass for fourteen hours a day, plagued by rain and mosquitoes. In a fire fight, we'd shoot until our arms ached and our weapons were empty, then we'd charge the enemy with bayonets!"

Looking straight ahead, the Chief says nothing. Then after a deliberately long, slow drink, he finally said, "Yeah, it figures... all shore duty!"

ALL SECURE

General Joe Whigham was ordered by the Secretary of Defense to gather together a Navy Lieutenant and Captains from the Army, Marine Corps, and Air Force to discover why the services have such trouble communicating with each other. He began by saying that their first project task was to "secure" a certain building, and asked each of them to go home and prepare a list of steps for the project management plan and to bring them to the meeting the next morning.

The Navy turned out the lights and locked the doors.

The Army posted a guard.

The Marines stormed the building using fire, maneuver and close combat, killed everyone inside, and set up a defensive perimeter.

The Air Force took out a lease, with an option to buy.

THE GOOD SAMARITAN

Two Navy Seals boarded a quick shuttle flight out of Dallas, headed for Houston. One sat in the window seat, and the other sat in the middle seat.

Just before take-off a Marine Master Sergeant got on and took the aisle seat next to the two Seals. The Marine kicked off his shoes, wiggled his toes and was settling in when the Seal in the window seat said, "I think I'll get up and get a coke."

"No problem," said the Marine, "Since I'm sitting in the aisle seat, I'll get it for you."

While he was gone, the Seal picked up the Marine's shoe and spit in it.

When the Master Sergeant returned with the coke the other Seal said, "That looks good, I think I'll have one too."

Since he was already up the Marine obligingly went to fetch it, and while he was gone the Seal picked up the other shoe and spit in it. After a couple of minutes the Top returned with the drink, and they all sat back and enjoyed the short flight to Houston.

As the plane was landing, the Marine slipped his feet into his shoes and knew immediately what had happened.

"How long must this go on?" he asked. "This fighting between our groups? This hatred? This animosity? This spitting in shoes, and pissing in cokes?"

GUNFIGHTING

USMC Rules For Gunfighting

1. Be courteous to everyone, friendly to no one.

2. Decide to be aggressive enough, quickly enough.

3. Have a plan.

4. Have a back-up plan, because the first one probably won't work.

5. Be polite. Be professional. But, have a plan to kill everyone you meet.

6. Do not attend a gunfight with a handgun whose caliber does not start with a "4."

7. Anything worth shooting is worth shooting twice. Ammo is cheap. Life is expensive.

8. Move away from your attacker. Distance is your friend. (Lateral and diagonal movement are preferred.)

9. Use cover or concealment as much as possible.

10. Flank your adversary when possible. Protect yours.

11. Always cheat; always win. The only unfair fight is the one you lose.

12. In ten years nobody will remember the details of caliber, stance, or tactics. They will only remember who lived.

13. If you are not shooting, you should be moving, communicating and reloading.

14. Someday someone may kill you with your own gun, but they should have to beat you to death with it because it is empty.

15. Above all ... don't drop your guard.

Navy Rules For Gunfighting

1. Go to Sea
2. Drink Coffee
3. Buy some candy at the gedunk
4. Send the Marines

Army Rules For Gunfighting

1. Select a new beret to wear
2. Sew combat patch on right shoulder
3. Reconsider the color of beret you decided to wear
4. Send the Marines

Air Force Rules For Gunfighting

1. Have a cocktail
2. Adjust temperature on air-conditioner
3. Determine "what is a gunfight"
4. Send the Marines

AIR FORCE OATH

I (state your name), swear to sign away four years of my useless life to the UNITED STATES AIR FORCE because I know I can't hack it in the Army, because the Marines frighten me, and I am afraid of water over waist deep. I swear to sit behind a desk and take credit for the work done by others more dedicated than me who take their job seriously. I also swear not to do any form of real exercise, but promise to defend our bike-riding test as a valid form of exercise. I swear to uphold and defend the Constitution of the United States, even though I believe myself to be above that. I promise to walk around calling everyone by their first name because I know I'm not really in the military and I find it amusing to annoy the other services. I will have a better quality of life than those around me and will, at all times, be sure to make them aware of that fact. After completion of "Basic Training" (snicker) I will be a lean, mean, donut-eating, coffee drinking, lazy-boy sitting, civilian-wearing-blue-clothes, Chairborne Ranger. I will do no work unless someone is watching me (and it makes me look good), will annoy those around me, and will go home early every day. I consent to never being promoted (ever) and understand that all those whom I made fun of yesterday will probably outrank me tomorrow. So help me God.

_____   _____

Signature   Date

ARMY OATH

I, Rambo, swear to sign away four years of my mediocre life to the UNITED STATES ARMY because I couldn't score high enough on the ASVAB to get into the Air Force, I'm not tough enough for the Marines, and the Navy won't take me because I can't swim. I will wear camouflage every day and tuck my trousers into my boots because I can't figure out how to use blousing straps. I promise to wear my uniform 24 hours a day even when I have a date. I will continue to tell myself that I am a fierce killing machine because my Drill Sergeant told me I am, despite the fact that the only action I will see is a Court Martial for sexual harassment. I acknowledge the fact that I will make E-8 in my first year of service, and vow to maintain that it is because I scored perfect on my PT test. After completion of my Sexual.... er.... I mean "Basic Training," I will attend a different Army school every other month and return knowing less that I did when I left. On my first trip home after boot camp, I will walk around like I am cool and propose to my 9th grade sweetheart. I will make my wife stay home because if I let her out she might leave me for a better looking Marine. Should she leave me twelve times, I will continue to take her back. While at work, I will maintain a look of knowledge while getting absolutely nothing accomplished. I will arrive to work every day at 1000 hours because of morning PT, and leave every day at 1300 to report back to "Company." I understand that I will undergo no training whatsoever that will help me get a job upon separation, and will end up working construction with my friends from high school. I will brag to everyone about the Army giving me $30,000 for college, but will be unable to use it because I can't pass a placement exam. So help me God.

_____   _____

Signature   Date

NAVY OATH

I, Top Gun, in lieu of going to prison, swear to sign away four years of my life to the UNITED STATES NAVY because I want to hang out with Marines without actually having to *be* one of them, because I thought the Air Force was too "corporate," because I didn't want to actually live in dirt like the Army, and because I thought, "Hey, I like to swim... why not?" I promise to wear clothes that went out of style in 1976 and to have my name stenciled on the butt of every pair of pants I own. I understand that I will be mistaken for the Good Humor Man during summer and for Nazi Waffen SS during the winter. I will strive to use a different language than the rest of the English-speaking world, using words like "deck, bulkhead, cover, geedunk, scuttlebutt, scuttle and head," when I really mean "floor, wall, hat, candy, water fountain, hole in wall, and toilet." I will take great pride in the fact that all Navy acronyms, rank, and insignia, and everything else for that matter, are completely different from the other services and make absolutely no sense whatsoever. I will muster, whatever that is, at 0700 hours every morning unless I am buddy-buddy with the Chief, in which case I will show up around 0930 hours. I vow to hone my coffee cup handling skills to the point that I can stand up in a kayak being tossed around in a typhoon, and still not spill a drop. I consent to being promoted and subsequently busted at least twice per fiscal year. I realize that once selected for Chief, I am required to submit myself to the sick, and quite possibly illegal whims of my newfound "colleagues." So help me Neptune.

_____   _____

Signature   Date

MARINE CORPS OATH

I, (have someone recite your name for you), swear... uhhh........ high and tight…........ grunt…....... kill…….… cammies…........ ugh…........ Air Force women…..... OOORRAAHH! So help me Corps!

_____

Make Your Mark

WORLDS APART

In an effort to ensure proper training and readiness among the military services, Congress has approved the following changes to basic principles of recruit training:

Haircuts

Marines: Heads will be shaved.

Army: Stylish flat-tops for all recruits.

Navy: No haircut standard.

Air Force: Complete makeovers as seen on the *Oprah Winfrey Show*.

Training Hours

Marines: Reveille at 0500, train until 2000.

Army: Reveille at 0600, train until 1900.

Navy: Get out of bed at 0900, train until 1100, lunch until 1300, train until 1600.

Air Force: Awaken at 1000, breakfast in bed, train from 1100 to 1200, lunch at 1200, train from 1300 to 1400, nap at 1400, awaken from nap at 1500, training ceases at 1500.

Meals

Marines: Meals, Ready-to-Eat three times a day.

Army: One hot meal, two MRE's.

Navy: Three hot meals.

Air Force: Catered meals prepared by the Galloping Gourmet, Julia Child, Wolfgang Puck and Emeril Lagasse. All you can eat.

Leave And Liberty

Marines: None.

Army: Four hours a week.

Navy: Two days a week.

Air Force: For every four hours of training, recruits will receive eight hours of leave and liberty.

Protocol

Marines: Will address all officers as "Sir," and refer to the rank of all enlisted members when speaking to them (i.e., Sgt. Smith).

Army: Will address all officers as "Sir" unless they are friends, and will call all enlisted personnel "Sarge."

Navy: Will address all officers as "Skipper," and all enlisted personnel as "Chief."

Air Force: All Air Force personnel shall be on a first name basis with each other.

Decorations/Awards

Marines: Medals and badges are awarded for acts of gallantry and bravery only.

Army: Medals and badges are awarded for every bullet fired, hand grenade thrown, fitness test passed, and bed made.

Navy: Will have ships' engineers make medals for them as desired.

Air Force: Will be issued all medals and badges, as they will most likely be awarded them at some point early in their careers anyway.

Camouflage Uniforms

Marines: Work uniform, to be worn only during training and in field situations.

Army: Will wear it anytime, anywhere.

Navy: Will not wear camouflage uniforms, since they do not camouflage you on a ship. (Ship Captains will make every effort to explain this to sailors.)

Air Force: Will defeat the purpose of camouflage uniforms by putting blue and silver chevrons and colorful squadron patches all over them.

Career Fields

Marines: All Marines shall be considered riflemen first and foremost.

Army: It doesn't matter, all career fields promote to E-8 in first enlistment anyway.

Navy: Nobody knows. The Navy is still trying figure out what sailors in the ABH, SMC, BNC and BSN rates do anyway.

Air Force: Every recruit will be trained in a manner that will allow them to leave the service early to go on to higher paying civilian jobs.

A CLOSE SHAVE

A Marine Master Sergeant and a Navy Captain were sitting in the barbershop. They were both just getting finished with their shaves, when the barbers reached for some after-shave to slap on their faces.

The Captain shouted, "Hey, don't put that stuff on me! My wife will think that I've been in a whorehouse!"

The Top turned to his barber and said, "Go ahead and put it on. *My* wife doesn't know what the inside of a whorehouse smells like!"

CARD GAME

One day a handsome Marine, Santa Claus, a heterosexual sailor, and the Easter Bunny were playing a game of high stakes poker. The pot grew and grew, until it contained several thousand dollars. Suddenly the lights went out, and when they came back on the money was gone. Who took it?

The answer should be obvious. It was the Marine. There is **no such thing** as Santa Claus, the Easter Bunny, or a heterosexual sailor.

MAKING A MARINE

A sailor was walking home from work one day when he noticed a little boy sitting on the sidewalk.

The little boy was playing with a pile of shit. Curious, the sailor walked over to the little boy and asked him, "Why are you playing with a pile of shit?"

The little boy replied "I'm making a Marine."

The sailor, amused by this, ran back to his ship to get the Captain. Upon returning to the little boy, who was still playing with the pile of shit, the Captain asked "Son, what are you doing?"

The little boy looked up at him and said, "I'm making a Marine."

The Captain, being equally amused, sent the sailor back to get the NCOIC of the ship's Marine Detachment. When they arrived the Gunny saw the little boy, still playing with his pile of shit, and asked him, "Son, what are you doing?"

The little boy again replied, "I'm making a Marine."

"What! Why are you making a Marine out of shit?" asked the obviously appalled Gunny.

The little boy paused and responded, "Because I don't have enough shit to make a sailor!"

MISTAKEN IDENTITY

One day a little boy was touring a Navy ship with his parents when he got separated from them. After a while he began to worry that they wouldn't be able to find him, so he started searching. After about ten minutes of looking he turned the corner of a passageway, where he bumped into a sailor in dress whites.

The sailor could see that the kid was lost and frightened, and bent down to calm him. After a while the sailor took off his 'dixie cup' hat, put it on the boy's head, and said, "You wear that, while I go look for your parents." With that he left.

The boy sat and waited, and before long he realized that he had to go to the bathroom – bad. He noticed that there was a head across the passageway, so he went in and stood in front of the closest urinal and tugged at his zipper. It was stuck. He tugged and tugged, but it was no good.

The little boy was on the verge of tears when suddenly a Marine entered the head. The boy quickly turned to face him, pointed to his crotch and said, "Mister, would you please unzip my fly?"

The Marine took a step back and said, "What are you, queer or something?"

The boy wondered why this Marine, who didn't know him from Adam, would ask such a thing. And then it dawned on him. So the boy replied, "Oh, no sir. I'm not *really* a sailor. I just borrowed this hat!"

PEARLY GATES

When General George S. Patton died he found himself standing before the Pearly Gates awaiting admission to Heaven. Saint Peter was naturally there to greet him, and once the General had signed in he proceeded to direct him to his quarters.

"Straight down this road General, and left at the first intersection. Your barracks will be on your right." Patton heaved his duffel bag up onto his shoulder and stepped off, but after only a few steps he turned and came back.

"Are there any Marines here?" he asked. Patton's dislike of Marines was well known, and he had no intention of spending eternity in their company.

Saint Peter seemed genuinely surprised by the question. "Marines… in **Heaven**? You must be kidding. They're all in the other place, of course!"

That satisfied the General, and once again he headed off to find his billeting area. As he approached the first intersection he was about to turn left as instructed, but what he saw there made him throw his gear to the ground in disgust. There, directing traffic in the middle of the road, was a Marine sergeant in full dress blues. His uniform was immaculate, and the sergeant himself was tall, handsome, muscular and tanned – by all accounts a typical Marine. The General couldn't believe that *Saint Peter* would lie, and he stormed back to the Pearly Gates to confront him.

"I thought you said there were no Marines here!" he shouted, and went on to tell the Saint what he had seen.

"Oh *him*," the kindly Saint replied. "That's just God. He likes to *pretend* that he's a Marine!"

ARE YOU SURE?

A Marine walked into a bar, sat down and said, "Hey barkeep, have you heard the joke about the four sailors in a farmhouse?" Chairs scraped behind him, and four of the biggest, meanest guys in the bar stood up.

The biggest one said, "*We're* in the Navy. You sure you wanna tell that joke?"

The Marine smirked in disbelief and said, "Nah, I guess you're right. I don't want to have to explain it *four times*!"

PAY IS THE SAME

An Army grunt stands in the rain with a thirty-five pound pack on his back, a fifteen pound weapon in hand, after having marched twelve miles, and says, "This is shit!"

An Army Airborne Ranger stands in the rain with a forty-five pound pack on his back, a fifteen pound weapon in hand, after having jumped from an airplane and marched eighteen miles, and says with a smile, "This is *good* shit!"

A Navy SEAL lies in the mud, with a fifty-five pound pack on his back, a fifteen pound weapon in hand, after having had a ten mile swim to shore, a five mile crawl through swamps, and a twenty-five mile march in the jungle, at night, through enemy positions, and says with a grin, "This is *really* good shit."

A Recon Marine, up to his nose in the stinking, bug-infested mud of a swamp, with a sixty pound pack on his back and a fifteen pound weapon in each hand, after jumping from an aircraft at high altitude, into the ocean, swimming twelve miles to the shore, killing several alligators to enter the swamp, then crawling thirty miles through the brush to assault an enemy camp, says, "I *love* this shit."

An Air Force NCO sits in an easy chair in an air conditioned, carpeted office, with a sandwich in one hand and a soft drink in the other, and says, "My e-mail's out? What kind of shit is *this*?"

PLAY BALL

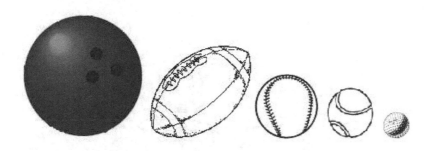

A survey was conducted to determine the favorite recreational activity within each of the armed services. Here are the results:

Marines: Bowling

Navy: Football

Army: Baseball

Coast Guard: Tennis

Air Force: Golf

Notice how the lower down you get, the smaller the balls are?

THE SENTRY

Two airmen were driving across the United States on leave when they came to a Marine Corps base. They decided to visit, and as they approached the gate the Marine Guard walked up to the driver's window and tapped on it with his nightstick. The driver rolled down the window, and the Marine smacked him in the head with the stick.

The driver said, "What did you do that for?"

The Marine replied, "You're on a United States Marine Corps Base, son. When I come up to your car, you'll have your ID card ready."

Driver said, "I'm sorry, we're in the Air Force, and we didn't know."

The Marine examined the I.D. card and gave it back to the driver. He then walked around to the passenger side and tapped on the window. The passenger rolled his window down, and the Marine smacked *him* with the nightstick.

The passenger said, "What'd you do that for?"

The Marine replied, "Just making your wish come true."

The passenger said, "Huh?"

The Marine answered, "I know, as soon as you pull away from the gate, you're gonna say, 'I wish that sucker would've tried that shit with *me*!'"

LEAVE A MESSAGE
PENTAGON ANSWERING MACHINE

We're sorry, but all of our units are deployed at the moment, or otherwise engaged. Please leave a message with your country, name of organization, region, specific crisis and a number where you can be reached. As soon as we have sorted out the Balkans, Iraq, Korea, Afghanistan, marching up and down the streets of Washington, D.C. and attending sexual harassment training, we will return your call.

Please speak after the tone, or if you require more options, please choose from the following menu:

- If your concern is distant, with a temperate climate and good hotels, and can be solved by one or two low-risk high-altitude bombing runs, press 1 for the

United States Air Force. Please note that this service is not available after 1630 hours, or on weekends. Special consideration will be given to customers requiring satellite or stealth technology who can provide additional research and development funding.

- If your inquiry concerns a situation which can be resolved by a bit of grey flannel, bunting, flags and a really good marching band, press 2 for the United States Navy. Please note that Tomahawk missile service is extremely limited and will be provided on a first-come, first-serve basis.

- If your inquiry is not urgent, press 3 for the United States Army.

- If you are in *really* big trouble, please press 4 and your call will be answered by the United States Marine Corps.

- If you are interested in joining the armed forces, and wish to be shouted at, paid little, have premature arthritis, put your family in a condemned hut miles from civilization, and are prepared to work your ass off, risking your life in all types of weather and terrain, both day and night, while watching Congress erode your original benefits package, then please stay on the line. Your call will be answered shortly by the next available bitter, passed-over for promotion recruiter located in the strip mall down by the post office.

Have a pleasant day, and thank you again for trying to contact the United States Armed Forces!

PERSONAL HYGIENE

A Marine and a sailor went into an airport restroom, and both took a leak. After using the head the Marine walked out, but the sailor stopped and washed his hands.

When he was done the sailor left the restroom and walked up to the Marine and told him, "In the Navy they taught us to wash our hands after we took a leak."

The Marine replied, "Well, is that right? In the Marines, they taught us not to piss on our hands!"

GIMME A BREAK

Active duty Marines frequently ask those of us who are retired what we do to make our days interesting.

I'll give you an example. I went to the Marine Corps Exchange the other day to pick up a package of batteries. I was only in there for about five minutes.

When I came out there was an MP standing there writing out a parking ticket.

I went up to him and said, "Come on buddy, don't be a jerk. How about giving a retiree a break?"

He ignored me and continued writing the ticket.

I called him a bad name. He glared at me and started writing another ticket for having worn tires.

So I called him a *way* worse name. He finished the second ticket and put it on the windshield with the first.

Then he started writing a third ticket.

This went on for about twenty minutes. The more I abused him, the more tickets he wrote.

But I didn't care. My car was parked around the corner, and this one had a "GO NAVY" bumper sticker on it.

CLIPPED WINGS

Three men died and went to heaven. One was a Marine, one was a Navy SEAL, and the third was an Army Ranger. When the trio arrived at the Pearly Gates, Saint Peter was at first unsure if he was going to let them in due to their history of philandering and boorish ways.

After some thought the Saint decided to admit them, but he also gave a strict warning for them not to have impure thoughts or they would lose their wings and burn in hell. All three men agreed, and walked through the gate.

As a test Saint Peter then sent a beautiful blonde angel walking seductively in front of them, and as she bent over and grabbed her ankles the Marine and the Ranger couldn't help but notice her shapely behind and immediately lost their wings.

Then, as the two men bent over to pick up their wings, the Navy SEAL took one look at *their* butts, and lost *his!*

BONUS BABIES

The Pentagon recently found it had too many generals, and as a result offered an early retirement bonus. They promised any general who retired immediately full annual benefits, plus $10,000 for every inch measured in a straight line between any two points on the general's body - with the general getting to select any pair of points he wished.

The first man, an Air Force general, accepted. He asked the pension man to measure from the top of his head to the tip of his toes. It was six feet, and he walked out with a check for $720,000.

The second man, an Army general, asked them to measure from the tip of his outstretched hands to his toes. It was eight feet, and he walked out with a check for $960,000.

When the third general, a grizzled old Marine, was asked where to measure, he told the pension man, "From the tip of my penis to the bottom of my testicles."

The pension man suggested that perhaps the Marine general might like to reconsider, pointing out the nice checks the previous two generals had received.

The Marine insisted, and the pension expert said that would be fine but that he'd better get the medical officer to do the measuring. The medical officer attended, and asked the general to drop 'em – so he did. The medical officer placed the measuring tape on the tip of the general's penis and began to work back.

"My God!" he said. "Where are your testicles?"

The general replied, "Vietnam."

THE BRAVEST

One day an Army general, a Navy admiral, and a Marine Corps general were having an argument about whose branch of the military was the bravest.

Suddenly the admiral yelled to a passing sailor, "Sailor, catch that falling anchor!"

The sailor snapped to attention, shouted, "Yes, sir!," ran under the anchor, and was crushed to death trying to catch it. The admiral turned to the others and said, "Gentlemen, that was bravery."

The Army general said, "That's nothing," and yelled, "Private, stop that moving tank!"

The private snapped to attention, shouted, "Yes, sir!" and was crushed under the tank while trying to stop it. The Army general turned back to the others and said, "Gentlemen, that took guts."

Finally, the Marine general took his turn. "Marine, tell these officers that soldiers and sailors are braver than Marines."

The Marine snapped to attention and shouted, "Screw you, sir!"

The Marine general turned to the others and said, "Now, gentlemen, *that* took balls!"

To Err Is Human, To Forgive Divine

OFFICER'S CALL

"The only thing more dangerous than a Second Lieutenant with a map and a compass is a Major with a word processor and a fax machine!"

To Err Is Human, To Forgive Divine

SEEING STARS

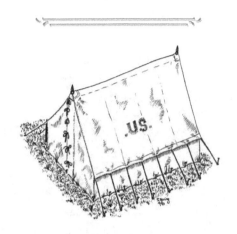

The Company Commander and the Gunny were in the field. As they hit the sack for the night, the Gunny said: "Sir, look up into the sky and tell me what you see?"

The C.O. said "I see millions of stars."

The Gunny then asked, "And what does that tell you, sir?"

The C.O. replied, "Astronomically, it tells me there are millions of galaxies and potentially billions of planets. Theologically, it tells me God is great, and that we are all small and insignificant. Meteorologically, it tells me we will have a beautiful day tomorrow. What does it tell you, Gunny?"

The Gunny slowly shook his head and said, "Well sir, it tells *me* that somebody stole our tent!"

CAN YOU HEAR ME NOW?

Having just moved into his new office, a pompous new colonel was sitting at his desk when a lance corporal knocked on the door. Conscious of his new position, the colonel quickly picked up the telephone, told the lance corporal to enter, and then said into the phone, "Yes, General, I'll be seeing him this afternoon and I'll pass along your message. In the meantime, thank you for your good wishes, sir." Feeling as though he had sufficiently impressed the young enlisted man, he asked, "What do you want, Marine?"

"Nothing important, sir," the lance corporal replied, "I'm just here to hook up your telephone."

PULLING RANK

During a field training exercise a lieutenant was driving down a muddy back road when he encountered another vehicle stuck in the mud - with a red-faced colonel at the wheel.

"Is your jeep stuck, sir?" asked the lieutenant as he pulled alongside.

"Nope," replied the colonel, coming over and handing him the keys, "Yours is!"

HELPING HAND

A sixty-ish stockbroker was walking down Wall Street one evening when he spotted a pan-handler, a somewhat younger man, in battered Vietnam-era fatigues. As he passed the guy, the broker dropped a couple of dollars in the man's cup and asked, "You were in the 'Nam?"

The panhandler looked up, said "Yes," and then paused. He looked closely at the broker, and said, "Major Smith? It's me, Corporal Wilson!"

"My God… Wilson! What the hell are you doing here?"

"Well sir, after I got out of the Corps nothing seemed to go right for me. I drank too much, couldn't hold a job, and got into trouble. But I'm okay now. Folks help out." He paused, and then said, "Major, you look great!"

"I got out as a lieutenant colonel. Went into the market, and I've been doing really well for myself."

Wilson said, "Well that's great sir. You have a great day. And thanks."

The Colonel started to walk off. Then he stopped for a second, thinking. He turned around and said, "Wilson, you were the best orderly I ever had. I'm a rich man now. Let me help you out."

"Sir?"

"Look, come work for me. You can be my valet. I've got a big house in mid-town, with plenty of room, and my wife won't mind."

"Sir, I really don't want to be a problem."

"No problem, and you'll just be doing the same sort of thing you did when we were back in the 'Nam. You know, keeping my stuff in order, making sure I'm up in the morning - just like in the old days."

"Okay, sir."

So the Colonel hailed a cab and the two piled in. On route uptown, they stopped at a men's shop and the Colonel bought Wilson some good civilian clothes. Then he took him out for lunch, where they had a few drinks and talked about old times.

They eventually got to the Colonel's house, a large brownstone in the East 60s, fairly late that evening. The Colonel gave Wilson a little tour, showed him where various things were stored, gave him a room, and said, "I'll see you in the morning."

At 0400, Wilson woke up, and at precisely 0415 he opened the door to the master bedroom, walked in, smacked the Colonel's wife on the behind and said, "Okay baby, here's five bucks, time to get back to the 'ville!"

BUTTER BAR

A young Second Lieutenant approached a crusty old Master Sergeant and asked him about the origin of the commissioned officer insignias.

"Well, Lieutenant, it's history and tradition. First, we gave you a gold bar representing that you're valuable BUT malleable. The silver bar of a First Lieutenant represents value, but less malleable. When you make Captain you're twice as valuable, so we give you two silver bars. As a Colonel, you soar over military masses, hence the eagle. And as a General, you're obviously a star. Does that answer your question?"

"Yes, Master Sergeant," replied the Lieutenant, "but what about Majors and Lieutenant Colonels?"

The Master Sergeant explained, "Now that goes waaaaaay back in history, back to the Garden of Eden even. You see, we've always made it a rule to cover our pricks with leaves!"

PROPER UNIFORM

A Marine lieutenant was being court-martialed for an incident where he was found chasing a young lady through the hallways of the hotel in which they were both staying. As it happened, neither of them was wearing any clothes. As a result, one of the charges against him was for "being out of uniform."

The officer's lawyer argued that the lieutenant was *not* out of uniform, as the regulations read: "Naval officers must be at all times appropriately attired for the activity in which they are engaged."

The lieutenant was acquitted.

MORNING BRIEFING

The Commanding Officer of a Marine Corps Regiment was about to start the morning briefing to his Staff & Battalion Commanders. While waiting for the coffee machine to finish its brewing, he decided to pose a question to all assembled. He explained that his wife had been a bit frisky the night before and as a result he had failed to get his usual amount of sound sleep. He posed the question of just how much of sex was "work" and how much of it was "pleasure"?

The XO chimed in by saying it was 75-25% in favor of work.

A Captain said it was 50-50%.

The Colonel's Aide, a Lieutenant., responded with 25-75% in favor of pleasure, depending on his state of inebriation at the time.

There being no consensus, the Colonel turned to the PFC who was in charge of making the coffee. What's YOUR opinion, Marine?

With no hesitiation, the young PFC responded, "Sir, it *has* to be 100% pleasure."

The Colonel was surprised, and asked him why.

"Well sir," began the PFC, "if there was *any* work involved, the officers would have me doing it for them!"

LAND NAVIGATION

One day three senior officers were out hiking and unexpectedly came upon a large, raging, violent river. They needed to get to the other side, but had no idea of how to do so.

The Air Force Colonel called out to God, and prayed, "Please God, give me the strength to cross this river."

POOF! God gave him big arms and strong legs, and he was able to swim across the river. It did, however, take him about two hours, and he almost drowned a couple of times.

Seeing this, the Army Colonel prayed to God, saying, "Please God, give me the strength and the tools to cross this river."

POOF! God gave him a rowboat. He was able to row across the river in about an hour, but it was rough, and he almost capsized the boat a couple of times.

The Navy Captain had seen how things worked out for the other two, so when he prayed to God, he said, "Please God, give me the strength, the tools, and the intelligence to cross this river."

POOF! God turned him into a Marine Lance Corporal... so he looked at the map, hiked upstream a couple of hundred yards, and walked across the bridge...

CIVILIAN SECTOR

Tom retired from the Marine Corps in his early fifties and started a second career, but even though he loved his new job he just couldn't seem to get to work on time. Every day he was five, ten, or even fifteen minutes late - but he was a good worker and really sharp, so his boss was in a quandary about how to deal with it.

Finally one day his boss called him into the office for a talk.

"Tom, I must tell you, I truly like your work ethic, you do a bang-up job... but being late for work nearly every day is quite annoying to me as well as your fellow workers."

Tom replied, "Yes boss, I know. I'm sorry, but I am working on it."

"That's what I like to hear," his boss said. "However, the fact that you consistently come to work late does puzzle me because I understand that you retired from the United States Marine Corps, and from what I hear they have some pretty rigid rules about tardiness. Isn't that correct?"

"Yes. I did retire from the Marine Corps, and I'm mighty proud of it!" said Tom.

"Well," continued the boss, "what did *they* say when you came in late?"

"They said, 'Good morning, General!'"

SWING WITH THE WING

"Flyin' low and feelin' mean,
Spot a family by a stream,
Drop some nape' and watch 'em scream,
Cause napalm sticks to kids!"

- Politically incorrect PT cadence from "An Officer and a Gentleman"

To Err Is Human, To Forgive Divine

WHAT TIME IS IT?

On some air bases the Air Force is on one side of the field and civilian aircraft use the other side, with the control tower in the middle.

One day the tower received a call from an aircraft asking, "What time is it?"

The tower responded, "Who is calling?"

The aircraft replied, "What difference does it make?"

The tower replied, "It makes a lot of difference. If you are an American Airlines flight, it is three o'clock. If you are an Air Force plane, it is 1500 hours. If you are a Navy aircraft, it is six bells. If you are an Army aircraft, the big hand is on the twelve and the little hand is on the three. And if I am speaking with a Marine Corps aircraft, it's Thursday afternoon and two hours until 'Happy Hour' at the officer's club!"

THE HERC & HORNET

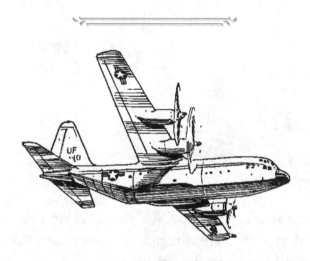

A couple of F/A-18 Hornets were escorting a C-130 Hercules, and their pilots were chatting with the pilot of the transport to pass the time. Eventually talk came 'round to the relative merits of their respective aircraft. Of course the fighter pilots contended that their airplanes were better because of their superior speed, maneuverability, weaponry, and so forth, while putting down the Herc's deficiencies in these areas.

After taking this for a while, the C-130 pilot said, "Oh yeah? Well, I can do a few things in this old girl that you'd only *dream* about." Naturally, the fighter jocks challenged him to demonstrate.

"Just watch," came the quick retort.

And so they watched… but all they saw was the C-130 continuing to fly straight and level.

After several minutes the Herc pilot came back on the air saying, "There! How was that?"

Not having seen anything, the fighter pilots replied, "What are you talking about? What did you do?"

And the Herc pilot answered, "Well, I turned on the autopilot, got up, stretched my legs, got a cup of coffee, and then went back and took a leak!"

FIGHTER PILOTS

Q: How do you know if there is a fighter pilot at your party?

A: He'll tell you.

Q. How do you know your date with the fighter pilot is half over?

A. He says, "But enough about me - wanna hear about my plane?"

Q: What's the difference between God and fighter pilots?

A: God doesn't think he's a fighter pilot.

Q: What's the difference between a fighter pilot and a jet engine?

A: A jet engine stops whining when the plane shuts down.

MR. FIX-IT
AIR WING MAINTENANCE LOGS

Some actual maintenance complaints submitted by military pilots... along with the replies from their maintenance crews...

PROBLEM: "Left inside main tire almost needs replacement."

SOLUTION: "Almost replaced left inside main tire."

PROBLEM: "Test flight okay, except autoland very rough."

SOLUTION: "Autoland not installed on this aircraft."

PROBLEM: "#2 Propeller seeping prop fluid."

SOLUTION: "#2 Propeller seepage normal. #1, #3, and #4 propellers lack normal seepage."

PROBLEM: "Something loose in cockpit."

SOLUTION: "Something tightened in cockpit."

PROBLEM: "Evidence of hydraulic leak on right main landing gear."

SOLUTION: "Evidence removed..."

PROBLEM: "DME volume unbelievably loud."

SOLUTION: "Volume set to more believable level."

PROBLEM: "Dead bugs on windshield."

SOLUTION: "Live bugs on order."

PROBLEM: "Autopilot in altitude hold mode produces a 200 fpm descent."

SOLUTION: "Cannot reproduce problem on ground."

PROBLEM: "IFF inoperative."

SOLUTION: "IFF is always inoperative in OFF mode."

PROBLEM: "Friction locks cause throttle levers to stick."

SOLUTION: "That's what they're there for."

PROBLEM: "Number three engine missing."

SOLUTION: "Engine found on right wing after brief search."

To Err Is Human, To Forgive Divine

OUR "ALLIES"

"You can never surrender too early, or too often."

- Rule of French warfare

To Err Is Human, To Forgive Divine

OUI, OUI!

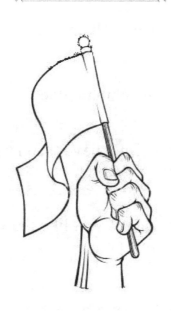

Q: What does the new French flag look like?

A: A white cross emblazoned on a white background!

Q: You are approached by three men while walking down a dark city street. One is British, one is American, and one is French. They all seem intent on mugging you. You have a gun, but alas, only two bullets. What do you do?

A: Shoot the Frenchman twice!

Q: What was the real reason the French didn't want the U.S. to attack Iraq?

A: They didn't want their record for surrender broken.

Q: How many Frenchman does it take to guard Paris?

A: Nobody knows… it's never been tried before!

Raise your right hand if you like the French ... raise *both* hands if you *are* French.

A French rifle is for sale on E-bay. It's never been fired, and has only been dropped once.

A GOOD IDEA

During one of the many wars that the French and the British fought (and the French usually lost), the French just happened to capture a British major. An officer brought the major to the French general for interrogation, and the French general began ridiculing the Major for wearing "that stupid red tunic." The French general finally asked, "Why do you wear that red uniform? It makes it easy for us to shoot you."

The British major replied, "If I do get wounded the blood will not show, and my soldiers will not get scared."

The French general said, "That is a very good idea!" He then turned to his orderly and said, "From now on, all French officers will wear brown pants!"

MARINES

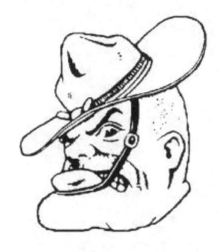

"There are only two types of people who understand Marines – the Marines themselves, and the enemy. Everyone else has a second hand opinion."

THE OLD SALT

Back in 1775, at Tun Tavern, recruiting started for the newly formed Marine Corps. The very first Marine enlistee came in, signed the papers, and took an oath. He was then told to go outside and wait for the other enlistees to go through the process, after which they would assemble on the front yard.

After a few minutes the second enlistee came out and had a seat on the steps beside the first. The first man looked at the second and began, "Son, let me tell you about the *Old* Corps..."

NEVER AGAIN

"Well," snarled the tough old Gunnery Sergeant to the bewildered young Private. "I suppose after you get discharged from the Corps, you'll just be waiting for me to die so you can come and piss on my grave."

"Not me, Gunny!" the Private replied. "Once I get out of the Marine Corps, I'm never going to stand in line again!"

GIVE HIM A MEDAL

As a crowded airliner was about to take off, the peace was shattered by a five-year-old boy who picked that moment to throw a wild temper tantrum. No matter what his frustrated, embarrassed mother did to try to calm him down the boy continued to scream furiously and kick the seats around him. Suddenly, from the rear of the plane, a man in a Marine Corps uniform was seen slowly walking forward up the aisle.

Stopping the flustered mother with an upraised hand, the courtly, soft-spoken Marine leaned down and, motioning toward his chest, whispered something into the boy's ear. Instantly the boy calmed down, gently took his mother's hand, and quietly fastened his seat belt. All the other passengers burst into spontaneous applause, and as the Marine slowly made his way back to his seat one of the cabin attendants touched his sleeve.

"Excuse me, sir," she asked quietly, "but could I ask you what magic words you used on that little boy?"

The Marine smiled serenely and gently confided, "I showed him my jump wings, service stars, and battle ribbons, explained that they entitle me to throw one passenger out the plane door on any flight I choose, and told him that I was just about to make my selection for this flight!"

THE OTHER PLACE

A Marine died in combat and woke up to find he was in hell. Naturally, he was really depressed as he stood in the processing line waiting to talk to an admittance counselor. He thought to himself, "I know I led a wild life, but hell, I'm a Marine. We're expected to live wild lives. I wasn't that bad. I never thought it would come to this." Looking up he saw that it is his turn to be processed into hell, so with fear and heavy heart he walked up to the counselor.

Counselor: "What's the problem, you look depressed?"

Marine: "Well, what do you expect? I'm in hell!"

Counselor: "Hell's not so bad. We actually have a lot of fun. Do you like to drink?"

Marine: "Of course I do. I'm a Marine."

Counselor: "Well then, you are going to love Mondays. On Mondays we drink up a storm. You can have whiskey, rum, tequila, beer, whatever you want, and as much you want. We party all night long. You'll *love* Mondays. Do you smoke?"

Marine: "Yes, as a matter of fact I do."

Counselor: "You are going to love Tuesdays. Tuesday is smoking day. You get to smoke the finest cigars and best cigarettes available anywhere. And you smoke to your heart's desire without worrying about cancer, because you are already dead! Is that great or what? You are going to *love* Tuesdays."

Counselor: "Do you like to fight?"

Marine: "Of course I do. I'm a Marine!"

Counselor: "You are going to love Wednesdays. That's Fighting Day. We challenge each other to fights to see who's the toughest in Hell. You don't have to worry about getting hurt or killed, because you're already dead. You are going to *love* Wednesdays. Do you gamble?"

Marine: "Show me a Marine who doesn't!"

Counselor: "You are going to love Thursdays, because we gamble all day and night. Black jack, craps, poker, slots, horse races, everything! You are going to love Thursdays. Are you gay?"

Marine: "Of course not! I'm a Marine!"

Counselor: "Oh….. well, you're going to *hate* Fridays!"

CHICKEN RANCH

An old Gunny finally retired from the Marine Corps and got the chicken ranch he had always wanted. He took with him his lifelong companion, a pet parrot he had acquired while on embassy duty in South America.

The first morning at 0430, the parrot squawked and said, "Reveille, reveille, reveille!" as was his habit.

The old Gunny rolled over and told the parrot, "We aren't in the Marine Corps anymore. Stop that and go back to sleep."

The next morning, which was to be the grand opening of the chicken ranch, the old Gunny awoke to a loud commotion. He jumped up from his rack and discovered the parrot was missing from his perch. Just then another screech was heard from the direction of the hen houses, so the Gunny threw on some clothes and ran outside to see what was going on.

When he approached the first hen house the Gunny saw dozens of his black chickens running around screaming. Some were missing feathers, and several lay unconscious on the ground. "What the hell is going on," he thought as he sprinted to the next hen house.

When the Gunny rounded the corner he found his white chickens in a similar state. Bloody chickens staggered about, and it looked as if the area had been struck by a cyclone.

He then raced to the third and final hen house, and as he rounded the corner he saw all of his brown chickens standing in formation with their head and eyes straight to the front. The parrot was pacing back and forth in front of them with a tiny DI cover perched on his head bellowing, "By God, when I say fall out in khaki, I mean *khaki!*"

HIGH EXPECTATIONS

While talking to a potential recruit, the Marine recruiter said, "Exactly what kind of job are you looking for in the Corps?"

The high school kid said, "I'm looking for something with an enlistment bonus of about $20,000, where I won't have to work too hard, and won't have to deploy overseas.

The recruiter said, "Well, what if I could hook you up with a skill that allowed you to come straight in at a pay grade of E-7, where you'll only work weekdays, and you can have any base of your choice and stay there as long as you want?"

The young recruit sat up straight and said, "Wow! Are you kidding?"

The recruiter replied, "Yeah, but you started it!"

UPTIGHT COLONEL

A crusty old Marine Corps Colonel found himself at a gala event at a posh hotel, sponsored by a local liberal arts college. There was no shortage of extremely attractive, idealistic young women in attendance, and it wasn't long before one of them approached the colonel.

"Excuse me sir, but you seem to be a very serious man. Are you this way all the time? Or is there something that's bothering you?"

"No, I'm just serious by nature."

Looking over the colonel's ribbons, the young lady said, "You seem to have seen a lot of action."

"Yes, a lot of action," said the colonel rather curtly.

Finding it hard work trying to start a conversation with the colonel, the young woman said, "You know, you should lighten up a little... relax and enjoy yourself."

This didn't seem to move the colonel, who just looked at her very seriously.

Exasperated, the woman said, "You know, I hope you don't take this the wrong way, but when was the last time you had sex?"

"1955," he replied."

"Well no wonder you're the way you are! You really need to chill out a little and quit taking everything so seriously. I mean, no sex since 1955 is a little extreme!"

"I don't think so – it's only 2130 now..."

MORAL OF THE STORY

A teacher gave her fifth grade class an assignment to get their parents to tell them a story with a moral at the end of it. The next day the kids came back and one by one began to tell their stories.

Kathy said, "My father's a farmer and we have a lot of egg-laying hens. One time we were taking our eggs to market in a basket on the front seat of the pickup when we hit a bump in the road and all the eggs went flying and broke and made a mess."

"And what's the moral of the story?" asked the teacher.

"Don't put all your eggs in one basket!"

"Very good," said the teacher. "Now, Lucy?"

"In our family we are farmers too. But we raise chickens for the meat market. We had a dozen eggs one time, but when they hatched we only got ten live chicks. And the moral to this story is, 'don't count your chickens until they hatch.'"

"That was a fine story Lucy. Johnny, do you have a story to share?"

"Yes, ma'am, my daddy told me this story about my Uncle Bill. Uncle Bill was a Marine fighter pilot in Desert Storm, and when his plane got hit he had to bail out over enemy territory. All he had on him was a bottle of whiskey, a machine gun and a machete. He drank the whiskey on the way down so the bottle wouldn't break, and then he landed right in the middle of one hundred enemy troops. He killed seventy of them with the machine gun until he ran out of bullets, then he killed twenty more with the machete till the blade broke, and then he killed the last ten with his bare hands."

"Good heavens," said the horrified teacher, "What kind of moral is there to *that* horrible story?"

"Don't screw with Uncle Bill when he's been drinking!"

BORN SALESMAN

Marine Corporal Ronald T. Jones was assigned to the induction center where he advised new recruits about their government benefits, especially their Serviceman's Group Life Insurance (SGLI).

It wasn't long before Captain Smith noticed that Corporal Jones was having a staggeringly high success rate, selling insurance to nearly 100% of the recruits he advised.

Rather than ask about this, the Captain stood in the back of the room and listened to Jones' sales pitch. Jones explained the basics of SGLI Insurance to the new recruits, and then said, "If you have SGLI Insurance and go into battle and are killed, the government has to pay $200,000 to your beneficiaries. If you *don't* have SGLI insurance and you go into battle and get killed, the government only has to pay a maximum of $6000."

"Now," he concluded, "which group do you think they are going to send into battle first?"

THE L.A. RIOTS

A True Story

Marines from Camp Pendleton were backing-up the Los Angeles Police Department on a call where someone had broken into a store. At the scene, the cops told the Marines to "cover" them as they approached the store (to police, "cover" means to point your weapons in the direction of the threat; but to Marines it means lay down a base of fire!). The Marines promptly laid down a base of fire, and fired 178 rounds before they stopped shooting. The thief, probably a little scared at this point, called 911 and reported, "They're *shooting* at me!"

ID PLEASE

A few years back one of the new Marines from the Barracks at Yorktown, Virginia was standing post at the main gate of the Naval Weapons Station. The duty policy was to check 100% of all ID cards including military in uniform, regardless of rank. A Navy sedan drove up to the gate with a young seaman at the wheel and a rear admiral sitting in the back. The young Marine PFC signaled for the car to stop, approached the driver, and asked to see both ID cards. The admiral told the Marine that he was on his way to meet with the station CO and didn't have time for such nonsense....

The admiral told the driver, "Go ahead."

The PFC told the driver, "Don't do that."

The admiral told the driver, "You heard me, drive on!"

The PFC asked the admiral as he drew his .45, "Sir, this is my first time on post. Do I shoot you, or your driver?"

The admiral showed his ID!

HOMEWORK

A fifth grade teacher told her class they were going to learn something about sex. She gave them an assignment to go home and learn something about it and come back the next day prepared to discuss it with the class.

The next day, the teacher asked, "Who has learned something about sex?"

No one said anything, except Little Johnny in the back of the room who had his hand up.

The teacher looked around again and this time called on Mary.

Mary said, "Well my parents thought I was asleep and they left their bedroom door open, and I saw my Daddy on top of my Mommy and she was yelling, 'Oh my God, Larry, I am coming!'"

The teacher said, "That's very good Mary, you learned something about sex, so you get an 'A' for class participation." The teacher looked around and called on Suzie next.

Suzie said, "My parents went out last night and they left me with my older sister. She had her boyfriend Jack come over. I snuck downstairs and hid and watched them. Jack pulled up my sister's skirt and ripped her panties off with his teeth."

The teacher said, "That's very good Suzie, you learned something about sex, and you also get an 'A' for class participation."

The teacher looked around and Johnny was busting a gut to tell his story, so finally she said, "Okay Johnny, tell us what you learned about sex."

Johnny said, "Well teach, it's like this. I went home last night and turned on the Fox News TV Channel, and there was story about a Marine in Afghanistan. There were Taliban to the north of him, Taliban to the south of him, Al Qaeda to the east of him, and Al Qaeda to the west of him - he was completely surrounded. This lone Marine quickly dug himself in, and with his M-16 and Desert Eagle he shot them all dead!"

The teacher looked amazed and said, "That's very interesting, but what does that have to do with *sex*?"

Johnny replies, "Just goes to show teach, don't f#ck with the Marines!"

DEAR MARINE

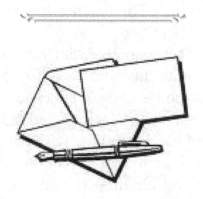

A Marine was deployed to Iraq, and while he was there he received a letter from his girlfriend. In the letter she explained that she had slept with two guys while he had been gone, and wanted to break up with him. She also said she wanted the picture he had of her back.

So the Marine did what any squared-away Marine would do. He went around to his buddies and collected all the unwanted photos of women he could find. He then mailed about twenty-five pictures of women (both with clothes, and without) to his girlfriend with the following note:

I don't remember which one you are. Please remove your picture and send the rest back.

– Semper Fi

HE IS GOD!

General

Leaps tall buildings with a single bound.
Is more powerful than a locomotive.
Is faster than a speeding bullet.
Walks on water.
Gives policy to God.

Colonel

Leaps short buildings with a single bound.
Is more powerful than a switch engine.
Is just as fast as a speeding bullet.
Walks on water if the sea is calm.
Talks with God.

Lieutenant Colonel

Leaps short buildings with a running start and favorable winds.
Is almost as powerful as a switch engine.
Is faster than a speeding B.B.
Walks on water in indoor swimming pools.
Talks with God if his special request chit is approved.

Major

Barely clears Quonset huts.
Loses tug of war with a locomotive.
Can fire a speeding bullet.
Swims well.
Is occasionally addressed by God.

Captain

Makes high marks when trying to leap building.
Is run over by locomotives.
Can sometimes handle a gun without self-injury.
Dog paddles.
Talks to animals.

First Lieutenant

Runs into buildings.
Recognizes locomotives two out of three times.
Is NOT issued ammunition.
Can stay afloat if properly instructed in the use of a
Mae West.
Talks to walls.

Second Lieutenant

Falls over doorsteps when trying to enter buildings.
Says: "Look at the choo-choo."
Wets himself with a water pistol.
Plays in mud puddles.
Mumbles to himself.

Sergeant

Lifts buildings and walks under them.
Kicks locomotives off the tracks.
Catches speeding bullets in his teeth.
Freezes water with a single glance.
HE IS GOD!!!

CHOSEN FROZEN

An Air Force C-130 was scheduled to leave Thule Air Base, Greenland at midnight. During the pilot's preflight check he discovered that the latrine holding tank was still full from the last flight, so a message was sent to the base and a Marine PFC who was there on an "exchange tour" - and was off duty - was called in to take care of it.

The young man finally got to the air base and made his way to the aircraft, only to find that the latrine pump truck had been left outdoors and was frozen solid - so he had to find another one in the hangar, which took even more time. He returned to the aircraft and was less than enthusiastic about what he had to do, but nevertheless went about the pumping job deliberately and carefully.

As he was leaving the plane the pilot stopped him and said, "Son, your attitude and performance has caused this flight to be late, and I'm going to personally see to it that you are not just reprimanded, but punished."

Shivering in the cold, his task finished, the PFC took a deep breath, stood up tall and said, "Sir, with all due respect, I'm not your son. I'm a United States Marine. I've been here in Greenland for eleven months without any leave, and reindeer are beginning to look pretty good to me. I only have one stripe. It's two-thirty in the morning, the temperature is forty degrees below zero, and my job is to pump shit out of your aircraft. Now just exactly what form of 'punishment' did you have in mind?"

RULES
FOR DATING A MARINE'S DAUGHTER

Rule One:

If you pull into my driveway and honk you'd better be delivering a package, because you're sure not picking anything or anyone up.

Rule Two:

You do not touch my daughter in front of me. You may glance at her, so long as you do not peer at anything below her neck. If you cannot keep your eyes or hands off of my daughter's body, I will remove them.

116

Rule Three:

I am aware that it is considered fashionable for boys of your age to wear their trousers so loosely that they appear to be falling off their hips. Please don't take this as an insult, but you and all of your friends are complete idiots. Still, I want to be fair and open minded about this issue, so I propose his compromise: You may come to the door with your underwear showing and your pants ten sizes too big, and I will not object. However, in order to ensure that your clothes do not, in fact, come off during the course of your date with my daughter, I will take my electric nail gun and fasten your trousers securely in place at the waist.

Rule Four:

I'm sure you've been told that in today's world, sex without utilizing a "barrier method" of some kind can kill you. Let me elaborate, when it comes to sex, *I* am the barrier, and *I* will kill you.

Rule Five:

It is usually understood that in order for us to get to know each other, we should talk about sports, politics, and other issues of the day. Please do not do this. The only information I require from you is an indication of when you expect to have my daughter safely back at my house, and the only word I need from you on this subject is "early."

Rule Six:

I have no doubt you are a popular fellow, with many opportunities to date other girls. This is fine with me as long as it is okay with my daughter. Otherwise, once you have gone out with my little girl, you will continue to date no one but her until she is finished with you. If you make her cry, I promise I will make *you* cry.

Rule Seven:

As you stand in my front hallway, waiting for my daughter to appear, and more than an hour goes by, do not sigh and fidget. If you want to be on time for the movie, you should not be dating. My daughter is putting on her makeup, a process that can take longer than painting the Golden Gate Bridge. Instead of just standing there, why don't you do something useful, like changing the oil in my car?

Rule Eight:

The following places are not appropriate for a date with my daughter: Places where there are beds, sofas, or anything softer than a wooden stool. Places where there are no parents, policemen, or nuns within eyesight. Places where there is darkness. Places where there is dancing, holding hands, or happiness. Places where the ambient temperature is warm enough to induce my daughter to wear shorts, tank tops, midriff T-shirts, or anything other than overalls, a sweater, and a goose down parka zipped up to her throat. Movies with a strong romantic or sexual theme are to be avoided; movies which feature chain saws are okay. Hockey games are okay. Old folks homes are better.

Rule Nine:

Do not lie to me. On issues relating to my daughter, I am the all-knowing, merciless god of your universe. If I ask you where you are going and with whom, you have one chance to tell me the truth, the whole truth and nothing but the truth. I have a shotgun, a shovel, and five acres behind the house. Do not trifle with me.

Rule Ten:

Be afraid. Be very afraid. It takes very little for me to mistake the sound of your car coming up the driveway for a chopper coming in over a rice paddy near Hanoi. When my Agent Orange starts acting up, the voices in my head frequently tell me to clean my guns as I wait for you to bring my daughter home. As soon as you pull into the driveway you should exit your car with both hands in plain sight. Speak the perimeter password, announce in a clear voice that you have brought my daughter home safely and early, and then return to your car - there is no need for you to come inside. The camouflaged face at the window is mine.

TACT

The Captain called the Company First Sergeant in and said, "First Sergeant, I just got notified by the Red Cross that Private Jones' mother died yesterday. Better go tell him, and send him in to see me."

So the First Sergeant called for morning formation and lined up all the troops. "Listen up, men," he said. "Johnson, report to the mess hall for mess duty. Smith, report to Personnel to sign some papers. The rest of you report to the Motor Pool for maintenance. Jones, your mother died, report to the commanding officer."

Later that day the Captain called the First Sergeant into his office again. "Hey, First Sergeant, that was a pretty cold way to inform Jones his mother died. Couldn't you be a bit more tactful next time?"

"Yes, sir," answered the First Sergeant.

A few months later, the Captain called the First Sergeant in once again with, "First Sergeant, I just got a telegram that Private McGrath's mother died. You'd better go tell him and send him in to see me. And this time, be more tactful."

"Aye aye, sir!"

So the First Sergeant called for morning formation. "Okay men, fall in and listen up. Everybody with a mother, take two steps forward. NOT SO FAST, McGrath!"

LIBERTY GUIDE

SYMPTOM: Feet cold and wet.

FAULT: Glass being held at incorrect angle.

ACTION: Rotate glass so that open end points toward ceiling.

SYMPTOM: Feet warm and wet.

FAULT: Improper bladder control.

ACTION: Stand next to nearest dog, complain about house training.

SYMPTOM: Opposite wall covered with fluorescent lights.

FAULT: It is the ceiling. You have fallen over backward.

ACTION: Have yourself lashed to the bar.

SYMPTOM: Mouth contains cigarette butts.

FAULT: You have fallen forward.

ACTION: See above.

SYMPTOM: Beer tasteless, front of your uniform is wet.

FAULT: Mouth not open, or glass applied to wrong part of face.

ACTION: Retire to head, practice in mirror.

SYMPTOM: Floor blurred.

FAULT: You are looking through bottom of empty glass.

ACTION: Get someone to buy you another beer.

SYMPTOM: Floor moving.

FAULT: You are being carried out.

ACTION: Find out if you are being taken to another bar.

SYMPTOM: Room seems unusually dark.

FAULT: Bar has closed.

ACTION: Confirm home address with bartender.

SYMPTOM: Taxi suddenly takes on colorful aspect and texture.

FAULT: Beer consumption has exceeded personal limitations.

ACTION: Cover mouth.

SYMPTOM: Beer is crystal-clear.

FAULT: It's water. Somebody is trying to sober you up.

ACTION: Punch him.

SYMPTOM: Hands hurts, nose hurts, mind unusually clear.

FAULT: You have been in a fight.

ACTION: Apologize to everyone you see, just in case it was them.

SYMPTOM: You don't recognize anyone, and don't recognize the room you're in.

FAULT: You've wandered into the wrong party.

ACTION: See if they have beer.

CINDERELLA LIBERTY

There were once three Marines who had a habit of going out and getting a bit juiced on paydays. One day their unit got a new Commanding Officer, and in reviewing the records of his men he was shocked to see what these three had been getting away with. So the CO ordered the Sergeant Major to have their heels locked in front of his office the next time they screwed up.

Sure enough it was payday, and all three came in a bit late. The Sergeant Major put them in clean uniforms, and had all three in front of the CO's office as he had been ordered.

When the first Marine reported, the CO chewed him out and asked why he had been late. The Marine told the CO he had gone on liberty, and when the bars closed he took a taxi back to base but it broke down, so he hitched a ride with an old man driving a horse drawn cart and just as they got near the gate the horse dropped dead and he had to walk the rest of the way in and therefore was late. The CO was skeptical, and told him to stand by in the passageway. He then called the second Marine in.

The CO told the second Marine that he had better give him an excuse he had never heard before or he would string him up to the yardarm. True to form the Marine told the same story as his buddy had about the broken down taxi, hitching a ride with an old man with a horse and cart, and the horse dropping dead. The CO went spastic and threatened to hang him. He then told the Sergeant Major to get number three in front of his desk, and by then he was really fired up. He asked the third Marine why he was late, and told him that he had *better* have a story he had never heard before.

Marine number three said he went on liberty and when the bars closed he caught a taxi back to the base... and suddenly the CO raised his hand and stopped him cold.

"Let me guess," the CO interrupted, "the taxi broke down?"

"No, sir," said the Marine, "for some reason there were dead horses all over the road, and it took us *forever* to get around them!"

TEMPTATION ISLAND

A newly married Marine was informed by headquarters that he was going to be stationed a long way from home on a remote island in the Pacific for a year. A few weeks after he got there he began to miss his new wife, so he wrote her a letter.

"My love," he wrote "we are going to be apart for a very long time. Already I'm starting to miss you, and there's really not much to do here in the evenings. Besides that, we're constantly surrounded by beautiful young native girls. Do you think if I had a hobby of some kind I would not be tempted?"

So his wife sent him back a harmonica saying, "Why don't you learn to play this?"

Eventually his tour of duty came to an end, and the Marine rushed back to his wife. "Darling." he said, "I can't wait to get you into bed so that we make passionate love!"

She kissed him and said, "First let's see you play that harmonica…"

NEVER ASK A GUNNY

A young Marine officer was in a serious car accident, but the only visible permanent injury was to both of his ears, which were amputated. Since he wasn't physically impaired he remained in the Marine Corps and eventually rose to the rank of General.

Despite his success, he was very sensitive about his appearance. One day the General was interviewing three Marines for his personal aide. The first was an aviator, and it was a great interview. At the end of the interview the General asked him, "Do you notice anything different about me?"

The young officer answered, "Why yes, sir. I couldn't help but notice that you have no ears." The general got very angry at the lack of tact, and threw him out.

The second interview was with a female lieutenant, and she was even better. The General asked her the same question, "Do you notice anything different about me?"

She replied, "Well, sir, you have no ears." The General threw her out also. The third interview was with a Marine Gunny. He was articulate, looked extremely sharp, and seemed to know more than the two officers combined.

The General wanted this guy, and went ahead with the same question, "Do you notice anything different about me?"

To his surprise the Gunny said, "Yes sir... you wear contacts lenses."

The General was very impressed and thought, 'what an incredibly observant Gunny, and he didn't even mention my ears.'

"And how do you know that I wear contacts?" the General asked.

The sharp-witted Gunny replied, "Well sir, it's pretty hard to wear glasses with no freaking ears!"

CAREER PATH

An old southern country preacher from Texas had a teenage son, and it was getting time for the boy to give some thought to choosing a profession.

Like many young men the boy didn't really know what he wanted to do, and he didn't seem too concerned about it.

One day, while the boy was away at school, his father decided to try an experiment. He went into the boy's room and placed on his study table four objects:

- a Bible
- a silver dollar
- a bottle of whisky
- a Playboy magazine

"I'll just hide behind the door," the preacher said to himself, "and when he comes home from school this afternoon, I'll see which object he picks up."

If it's the Bible, he's going to be a preacher like me, and what a blessing that would be! If he picks up the dollar, he's going to be a businessman, and that would be okay... but if picks up the bottle, he's going to be a no-good drunkard, and Lord what a shame that would be. And worst of all, if he picks up that magazine he's gonna be a skirt-chasin' bum."

The old man waited anxiously, and soon heard his son's footsteps as he entered the house whistling and headed for his room. The boy tossed his books on the bed, and as he turned to leave the room he spotted the objects on the table.

With curiosity in his eye, he walked over to inspect them. After thinking for a moment he picked up the Bible and placed it under his arm. He then picked up the silver dollar and dropped it into his pocket. Finally he uncorked the bottle and took a big drink while admiring the centerfold.

"Lord have mercy," the old preacher disgustedly whispered, "he's gonna be a Marine!"

HEAVEN CAN WAIT

The Pope died and went to heaven, and was stopped at the gate by a sleepy watchman who asked him, "Yeah, what do you want?"

The Pope thought, "Great! I did thirty years of God's work, only to get stopped by this guy." Then he said "Look, I am the Pope. I have done many years of good work."

The watchman said, "We ain't got no orders for you. Go get some rest and we'll see you in the morning." He then gave the Pope directions to an old World War II open bay barracks. The Pope went in to find all the lower bunks taken and the only lockers left have no doors, so he threw his gear under his rack and went to sleep.

The next morning the Pope was awakened by loud music and cheering. He ran to the window and saw a long black limo with a Marine Gunny in the back seat smoking a huge cigar, hanging on to a mug of Jack & Coke, and with two beautiful blond angels hanging on to him. The Pope was angry and went to the night watchman. He said, "I'm the Pope! I did thirty years of God's work at the Vatican, only to see some Marine Gunny - who probably did everything imaginable that a Marine might do - get treated like royalty!"

The watchman said, "There's a good reason for that. We get a Pope every twenty to thirty years. This is our first Marine Gunny ever!"

To Err Is Human, To Forgive Divine

POLITICALLY INCORRECT

"A committee of Congressmen, who asshole to asshole couldn't make a collective beer fart in a whirlwind..." - Mythical Gunnery Sergeant Tom Highway (as portrayed by Clint Eastwood) in the film "Heartbreak Ridge"

To Err Is Human, To Forgive Divine

COVERING HIS BUTT

News anchor Dan Rather, the Reverend Jesse Jackson, NPR reporter Cokie Roberts, and an American Marine were hiking through the jungle one day when they were captured by cannibals.

They were tied up, led to the village and brought before the chief.

The chief said, "I am familiar with your Western custom of granting the condemned a last wish. Before we kill and eat you, do you have any last requests?"

Dan Rather said, "Well, I'm a Texan... so I'd like one last bowlful of hot, spicy chili." The chief nodded to an underling, who left and returned with the chili. Rather ate it all and said, "Now I can die content."

Jesse Jackson said, "You know, the thing in this life I am proudest of is my work on behalf of the poor and oppressed. So before I go, I want to sing 'We Shall Overcome' one last time."

The chief said, "Go right ahead, we're listening." Jackson sang the song, and then said, "Now I can die in peace."

Cokie Roberts said, "I'm a reporter to the end. I want to take out my tape recorder and describe the scene here and what's about to happen. Maybe someday someone will hear it and know that I was on the job until the very end." The chief directed an aide to hand over the tape recorder, and Roberts dictated some comments. She then said, "Now I can die happy."

The chief turned and said, "And now, Mr. Marine, what is your final wish?"

"Kick me in the ass," said the Marine.

"What?" said the chief. "Will you mock us in your last hour?"

"No, I'm not kidding. I want you to kick me in the ass," insisted the Marine.

So the chief shoved him into the open, and kicked him in the ass. The Marine went sprawling, but rolled to his knees, pulled out a 9mm pistol he had hidden in his waistband, and shot the chief dead. In the resulting confusion he leapt to his knapsack, pulled out his M4 carbine, and sprayed the cannibals with gunfire. In a flash, the cannibals were dead or fleeing for their lives.

As the Marine was untying the others they asked him, "Why didn't you just shoot them? Why did you ask them to kick you in the ass first?"

"What!?" said the Marine. "And have you jerks call ME the aggressor!?"

SHREWD MOVE

When Bill Clinton was still President he returned to Washington after a weekend trip home to Arkansas, and stepped from his helicopter and onto the White House lawn carrying two Arkansas-bred hogs.

At the bottom of the steps a young Marine sergeant snapped to attention, saluted sharply and said, "Fine looking pigs, sir!"

Clinton turned and glared at the boy. "Son, don't you know I'm from Arkansas? These ain't pigs, they're *hogs.*"

The Marine replied, "This Marine begs the Commander In Chief's pardon, sir. Fine looking *hogs*, sir!"

Clinton smiled with pride, and the young man relaxed.

The President went on, "Thank you, son. You see this one here?" He nodded to the hog under his right arm. "I got this one for Chelsea." Then he nodded to the hog under his left arm. "This one here, I got for Hillary."

At that the Marine snapped back to attention and said, "Outstanding trades, sir!"

HAIL TO THE CHIEF

A few days after George W. Bush's inauguration, a man came up to the uniformed Marine on duty at the White House and said, "I'd like to see President Clinton."

The Marine politely answered, "Sir, Mr. Clinton is no longer President."

The man said, "Oh, okay," and walked away.

The next day the Marine was again on duty when the same man approached and again asked to see President Clinton.

The Marine again answered, "Sir, Mr. Clinton is no longer President."

Again the man answered, "Oh, okay," and walked away.

The next day the same man once again approached the same Marine and again asked to see President Clinton.

The Marine, by now a little annoyed, said "Sir, as I've told you several times, Mr. Clinton is no longer President. Don't you understand that?"

"Yes, I do," said the man, "but I just enjoy *hearing* it."

The Marine smiled, saluted the man smartly, and said, "Yes sir. See you tomorrow!"

AN UNDERSTANDING

A squad of Marines was driving up the highway between Basra and Baghdad when they came upon an Iraqi soldier who was badly injured and unconscious. Nearby, on the opposite side of the road, was an American Marine in a similar but less serious state. The Marine was conscious and alert, and as first aid was given to both men the Marine was asked what had happened.

He reported, "I was heavily armed and moving north along the highway when I spotted a heavily armed Iraqi soldier coming south."

"What happened then?" the corpsman asked.

"I yelled to him that, 'Saddam Hussein was a miserable piece of crap,' and he yelled back, 'John Kerry, Ted Kennedy and Bill Clinton are miserable pieces of crap.'"

"So is that when you started fighting with each other?"

"No... the two of us were just standing there shaking hands in the middle of the road when a truck hit us!"

SOBER UP!

During the Presidential Inauguration of 1992 a number of Marines were sent from Marine Barracks Eight & I to provide security and perform a number of ceremonial duties at a posh hotel which hosted a big party attended by the incoming president, Bill Clinton.

Being the squared away professionals that they were, the Marines performed their duties in an exemplary fashion, and as a reward the fellow running the event told them to make themselves at home and enjoy some of the free libations when their job was done - and that is exactly what they did.

Several hours later one of the sergeants from the detail, who was extremely inebriated, got into an elevator to find a new party to crash. By this time his uniform was a bit disheveled, but he didn't care.

Suddenly the elevator stopped, and when the doors opened he was joined by none other than Hillary Clinton, along with her Secret Service detail. The new First Lady took one look at the Marine and turned up her nose in disgust. The sergeant reeked of alcohol, and in any case it was a well known fact around Washington that Mrs. Clinton didn't like the military very much.

Finally Hillary could contain herself no longer. She turned to the sergeant and said, "Marine, you are *drunk!*"

The sergeant snapped to attention as best he could and replied, "Yes ma'am, I am. But tomorrow I'll be sober, and you'll *still* be ugly!"

GO NAVY!

"The only time the Navy and the Marine Corps are on the same side is in time of war, and during the Army - Navy game!" - The Great Santini

BEAT ARMY!

Q: Why do West Point graduates hang their diplomas from the rear view mirror?

A: To justify their handicapped parking.

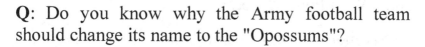

Q: Do you know why the Army football team should change its name to the "Opossums"?

A: Because they play dead at home and get killed on the road.

Q: Why doesn't Army have ice on the sidelines during games?

A: The guy with the recipe graduated.

Q. What do you get when you drive slowly by the West Point campus?

A. A degree.

Q: What do a Navy Midshipman and a West Point Cadet have in common?

A: They both got accepted to West Point.

Q: What do you get when you breed a groundhog and a West Point Cadet?

A: Six more weeks of bad football!

DEE-FENSE!

Navy was playing Army, and the cadets had a first down with three minutes left in the half. Suddenly an Army fan set off a firecracker and Navy, thinking it was the end of the half, ran off the field. Three plays later, Army punted!

CHEMICAL THREAT
ARMY FOOTBALL PRACTICE DELAYED

West Point (NY) – While preparing for tomorrow's Army-Navy Game, Army football practice was delayed for nearly two hours after a player reported finding an unknown powdery white substance on the practice field. The new head coach immediately suspended practice while police and federal investigators were called in to investigate.

After a complete analysis by both the FBI and Army Intelligence, forensic experts determined the powdery white substance unknown to players was the goal line.

Practice was resumed after special agents decided the team was unlikely to encounter the substance again.

BOOT CAMP

"Hell Private Joker, I like you. You can come over to my house and f**k my sister!"

- Drill Instructor Gunnery Sergeant Hartman in "Full Metal Jacket"

OVER THE HILL

As the sun rose over Parris Island, the senior drill instructor realized that one of his recruits had gone UA. A search party was dispatched immediately, and after a few hours the recruit was discovered hiding in some bushes. He was sent back to the base and promptly escorted to the drill instructor's office. The drill instructor asked the young recruit, "Why did you go UA, numb nuts?"

The recruit replied, "My *first* day here you issued me a comb, and then proceeded to cut my hair off. The *second* day you issued me a toothbrush, and sent me to the dentist, who proceeded to pull half my teeth. The *third* day you issued me a jock strap, and I wasn't about to stick around and find out what would follow that, SIR!"

TEN MINUTES

After a day of grueling field training under the blazing South Carolina sun, the platoon stood in front of their barracks at Parris Island. Their feet were covered with blisters, their backs ached from carrying heavy packs, and their stomachs growled since they hadn't eaten all day.

"All right, ladies, think about this," bellowed the drill instructor. "If you could have ten minutes alone, right now, with *anyone* in the world, who would it be?"

Amid much mumbling, one voice was heard from the rear rank. "Sir, my recruiter, sir!"

THE RECRUIT

The following is a letter from a farm kid now at MCRD San Diego:

Dear Ma and Pa:

I am well. Hope you are too. Tell Brother Walt and Brother Elmer the Marine Corps beats working for old man Minch by a mile. Tell them to join up quick before maybe all of the places are filled.

I was restless at first because you got to stay in bed till near six AM, but am getting so I like to sleep late.

Tell Walt and Elmer all you do here before breakfast is smooth your cot and shine some things. No hogs to slop, feed to pitch, mash to mix, wood to split, fire to lay. Practically nothin' else. Men got to shave, but it is not so bad – there's even warm water.

Breakfast is strong on trimmings like fruit juice, cereal, eggs, bacon, etc, but kind of weak on chops, potatoes, ham, steak, fried eggplant, pie and other regular food, but tell Walt and Elmer you can always sit by the two city boys that live on coffee. Their food plus yours holds you till noon when you git fed again.

It's no wonder these city boys can't walk much. We go on "route marches," which the platoon sergeant says are long walks to harden us. If he thinks so, it's not my place to tell him different. A "route march" is about as far as to our mailbox at home. Then the city guys get sore feet and we all ride back in trucks. The country here is nice, but awful flat.

The sergeant is like a school teacher. He nags a lot. The captain is like the school board. Majors and colonels just ride around and frown. They don't bother you none.

This next will kill Walt and Elmer with laughing. I keep getting medals for shooting. I don't know why. The bulls-eye is near as big as a chipmunk head and don't even move, and it ain't shootin' back at you like the Higgett boys at home. All you got to do is lie there all comfortable and hit it. You don't even load your own cartridges. They come in boxes.

Then we have what they call hand-to-hand combat training. You git to wrassle with them city boys. I have to be real careful though, they break real easy. It ain't like fightin' with that ole bull at home. I'm about the best they got in this 'cept for that Tug Jordan from over in Silver Lake. I only beat him once. He joined up the same time as me, but I'm only 5'6" and 130 pounds, and he's 6'8" and weighs near 300 pounds dry.

Be sure to tell Walt and Elmer to hurry and join before other fellers get onto this setup and come stampedin' in.

Your loving daughter,
Betty Lou

THERE'S ALWAYS ONE

As a group of recruits stood in formation at the Marine Corps Recruit Depot in Parris Island, the Drill Instructor said, "All right! All of you idiots, fall out!"

As the rest of the platoon sprinted away, one recruit remained where he was at the position of attention.

The Drill Instructor walked over until he was eye-to-eye with him, and then raised a single eyebrow. The recruit smiled and said, "Sure was a *lot* of 'em, huh, sir?"

TERRORISTS AND SUCH...

"There is no terrorist threat."

- "Film maker" Michael Moore (remember, this is a book full of jokes!)

To Err Is Human, To Forgive Divine

AMBUSH

An Iraqi battalion was on patrol when their commander noticed a lone Marine standing on a sand dune in their area.

Their Colonel told two of his soldiers to go take out the Marine, so they dropped their packs and promptly ran as fast as they could toward him - but just before they got to the top of the dune, the

171

Marine ran over to the other side. The two soldiers followed, and for the next few minutes there were bloody screams and dust flying in the air. Then as quickly as it had started it stopped, and the Marine came back up onto the dune. He brushed off his cammies, straightened his cover, crossed his arms and stood there looking at the Iraqis.

The infuriated Colonel then called for a *squad* to go get the Marine. They promptly ran as fast as they could toward him, but just before they got to the top the Marine ran over the other side of the dune once again. The Iraqi squad followed, and for the next few minutes there were more bloody screams and dust flying in the air. Then as quickly as it had started it stopped, and the Marine returned to the top of the dune. He brushed off his cammies, straightened his cover, crossed his arms and stood there looking at the Iraqis yet again.

The Iraqi Colonel was really hot now. He ordered an entire *company* to attack the Marine. Determined that the Republican Guards were far superior to one lone Marine, they had blood in their eyes as they ran up the sand dune. Once again, just before they got to the top, the Marine ran over to the other side of the dune. The bloodthirsty soldiers followed. For many minutes there were horrific screams and dust flying in the air. It continued and continued. Finally, one lone soldier came crawling back to the Colonel, all bloody and beaten about the head and shoulders. His uniform was torn, and there were cuts and bruises all over his body. The Colonel asked for a report.

The lone soldier, trying to catch his breath, replied in a trembling voice, "Sir,.. run,... it's a trick. There are TWO of them!!"

BAGHDAD ROSE

Two Marines in Iraq had just come back from a patrol and sat down to listen to the radio.

"American soldiers," cooed a soft female voice, "Your so-called national leaders have lied to you. You are needlessly risking your lives to wage a useless, unjust, illegal, and unwinnable war. Now is the time to return home to your loved ones, while you are still alive. If you foolishly insist on remaining where you are not wanted, the brave resistance fighters will have no choice but to kill you and add your name to the long and ever-increasing casualty list of this insane war. So why

risk never seeing your loved ones again for a so-
called president who has repeatedly lied and
deceived you at every opportunity? Why should you
be sacrificed so that U.S. corporations can enjoy
fatter profits? The only wise thing to do is return
home now, while you are still drawing breath,
before you return home zippered into a body bag."

"What's this?" sneered one Marine. "An Islamic-
terrorist version of Tokyo Rose?"

"No," answered the other. "It's just CNN!"

THE SADDAM BUNCH

Once sons Uday and Qusay were eliminated, many of Saddam Hussein's lesser-known relatives came to the attention of American authorities including:

Sooflay ....the restaurateur
Guday.........................the Australian half-brother
Huray.........................the sports fanatic
Sashay........................the gay brother
Kuntay & Kintay.....the twins by his African wife
Sayhay.......................the baseball player
Ojay...........................the stalker/murderer
Gulay.........................the singer/entertainer
Ebay..........................the internet czar
Biliray.......................the country music star
Ecksray.....................the radiologist
Puray.........................the gourmet chef
Regay.........................the Jamaican half-brother
Tupay........................the brother with the bad hair
Lattay........................the sister who works in Starbucks
Bufay.........................the chubby sister
Dushay.......................the very clean sister
Sapheway...................the sister who works in a grocery store
Ollay..........................the Mexican half-sister
Gudlay.......................the slutty sister

And finally, there is Oyvey, but the family doesn't like to talk about him…

BODY DOUBLES

An Iraqi general summoned Saddam's forty-eight body doubles to a safe house in Iraq.

"I have good news, and I have bad news" he told the doubles. "The good news is, Saddam is alive!"

Everybody in the room gave a big cheer... "Saddam! Saddam! Saddam! Saddam!"

The Iraqi General then turned to the doubles and said, "The *bad* news is, he's lost an arm..."

VALENTINE'S DAY

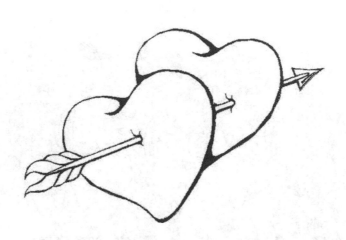

Little David came home from first grade one day and told his father that his class had just learned about the history of Valentine's Day.

"Since Valentine's Day is named for a Christian saint and we're Jewish," he asked, "will God get mad at me for giving someone a valentine?"

David's father thought about it a bit, and then said, "No, I don't think God would get mad. Who do you want to give a valentine to?"

"Osama Bin Laden," David said.

"Why Osama Bin Laden?" his father asked in shock.

"Well," David said, "I thought that if a little American Jewish boy could have enough love to give Osama a valentine, he might start to think that maybe we're not all bad, and maybe start loving people a little bit. And if other kids saw what I did and sent valentines to Osama, he'd love everyone a lot. And then he'd start going all over the place to tell everyone how much he loved them, and how he didn't hate anyone anymore."

The father's heart swelled and he looked at his boy with new found pride. "David, that's the most wonderful thing I've ever heard."

"I know," David said, "and once that gets him out in the open, the Marines can blow the *crap* out of that &*%$#@ing SOB!"

TERRORIST THREAT

This morning, from a cave somewhere in northern Pakistan, the Taliban Minister of Migration, Mohammed Omar, warned the United States that if military action against Afghanistan and Iraq continues, Taliban authorities will cut off America's supply of convenience store managers...

A NEW GAME

Three strangers struck up a conversation in a small airport passenger lounge in Dodge City, Kansas while awaiting their flight to Dallas. One was an American Indian who had driven over from Lamont, Colorado. The second was a retired Marine Gunnery Sergeant who had moved home to Texas and gone to work as a cowboy, and the third passenger was a fundamentalist Arab student from a Middle Eastern country hostile to America.

181

Their discussion drifted to their diverse cultures. Soon, the two Westerners learned by his crude conversational style that the Arab was indeed a devout radical Muslim activist, and the conversation rapidly fell into a very uneasy lull.

The old Marine leaned back in his chair, crossed his dusty cowboy boots on a magazine table, and tipped his big sweat-stained Stetson forward over his face - gracefully bowing out of any further aggravating conversation with the Arab student. The wind outside was blowing dust-devils around, and the old windsock was flapping... but still no plane came.

Finally, the American Indian cleared his throat and softly he spoke, "At one time here, my people were many, but sadly, now we are few."

The Muslim student raised an eyebrow and leaned forward, "Once my people were few," he sneered, "and now we are many. Why do you suppose that is?"

The Gunny shifted his toothpick to one side of his mouth and from the darkness beneath his Stetson said in a slow drawl, "That's 'cause we ain't played Cowboys and *Muslims* yet... but I do believe it's a-comin'!"

WHY WAIT?

Two friends named Sam and Bill joined the Marine Corps and were eventually sent to Iraq. While there they were put on street patrol in Baghdad, with instructions to enforce the military curfew which was in effect. There had been a lot of attacks by insurgents in recent days, so the two were told to shoot anybody who was on the streets after six PM.

One day they were patrolling their sector at twenty minutes to six, when Sam spotted a man walking on the other side of the street. Without a word, he lined up the man in his sights and shot him dead.

Bill was shocked, and said, "What are you doin', Sam? It ain't 6 o'clock yet!"

"I know what I'm doin' Bill," replied his trigger-happy buddy. "I know where that guy lives, and he *never* would have made it in time!"

TV SHOWS NO LONGER SEEN IN IRAQ

"Husseinfeld"

"Mad About Everything"

"Suddenly Sanctions"

"Matima Loves Chachi"

"Buffy the Slayer of Yankee Imperialist Dogs"

"Wheel of Misfortune and Terror"

"Iraq's Wackiest Public Execution Bloopers"

"Achmed's Creek"

"The Price is Right if Saddam *Says* It's Right"

"Veronica's Closet Full of Black, Shapeless Dresses"

"Two Guys, a Girl, and a Mosque"

"When Kurds Attack"

"Just Shoot Me"

"My Two Baghdads"

"Everybody Loves Saddam (Or He'll Have Them Shot)"

"Captured Iranian Soldiers Say the Darndest Things"

To Err Is Human, To Forgive Divine

SISTER SERVICES

*"There's a sailor (and sometimes a soldier) in the gay singing group 'The Village People' for a **reason**..."* - Unidentified Marine at Happy Hour

To Err Is Human, To Forgive Divine

LIBERTY CALL

An Army lieutenant gave his troops a few days off after a field exercise, so several decided to go down to Panama City Beach for some fun and relaxation. When the lieutenant saw the soldiers on their first day back he asked about the vacation.

"Not good sir," said one private. "We never made it to the beach."

"Why not," the lieutenant asked, "car trouble?"

"No," another replied. "Every few miles down the interstate we saw signs that said, 'Exit, Clean Restrooms.' We,, you have no idea how *many* restrooms we cleaned between Fort Benning and Panama City!"

MODERN CAVALRY

During the war in Afghanistan you may have seen footage on television showing Army Special Forces troops riding horses into combat alongside Afghan freedom fighters.

In a related story, an Army Ranger was almost killed in a tragic horseback riding accident. He fell from his horse, and was nearly trampled to death.

Thank God the manager of the K-Mart came out and unplugged it!

MONKEY BUSINESS

The San Diego Zoo had acquired a very rare species of gorilla. Within a few weeks, the female gorilla became very cranky and difficult to handle. Upon examination, the zoo veterinarian determined the problem. The gorilla was in heat, and to make matters worse, there were no male gorillas available.

While reflecting on their problem the zoo administrators noticed young Sam, the employee responsible for cleaning the animals' cages. Sam had recently gotten out of the Navy, and had spent a great deal of time at sea - so the zoo administrators thought they might have a solution.

Sam was approached with a proposition. Would he be willing to have sex with the gorilla for five hundred dollars?

Sam showed some interest, but said he would have to think the matter over carefully... and the following day announced that he would accept their offer - but only under three conditions.

"First," he said, "I don't want to have to kiss her. Secondly, I want nothing to do with any offspring that may result from this union."

The zoo administration quickly agreed to these conditions, and asked about the third.

"Well," said Sam, "you've gotta give me another week to come up with the five hundred dollars!"

DON'T ASK, DON'T TELL

Q: What do you call a sailor with a sheep under one arm and a goat under the other?

A: Bisexual!

GOOD DEED, BAD IDEA

An Air Force officer went to heaven, and when he arrived at the Pearly Gates Saint Peter asked him if he had ever done anything in his life which he believed would make him worthy of admittance to heaven.

The officer flyboy replied, "Yes, I once went into a bar with four of my pilot friends and saw a Marine harassing a young girl at the bar. Being a gentleman, I went up to him and told him to leave the young lady alone. When he refused I told him again more forcefully. This time I slapped him across the face and told the Marine to stand down."

Saint Peter said, "That was a very good thing to do. When did this happen?"

The pilot replied, "Oh, about five minutes ago. My friends should be here shortly!"

A CAMEL'S HUMP

A very respected Army captain was transferred to a remote desert outpost in Iraq, and on his orientation tour noticed a very old, seedy looking camel tied out behind the enlisted men's barracks. He asked the sergeant leading the tour, "Why is there a camel tied to the barracks?"

The sergeant replied, "Well sir, we're a long way from anywhere, and the men have natural sexual urges, so when they do... uh... we have the camel ready for them."

The captain said, "Well, I suppose if it's good for morale, then I guess it's all right with me."

After he had been stationed at the outpost for six long, lonely months, the captain simply couldn't control his sexual angst any longer. He barked to his sergeant, "Bring the camel into my tent!"

The sergeant shrugged his shoulders, looked at the other men, and led the camel into the captain's quarters. Within a few minutes the captain emerged from his tent fastening his trousers, and he was beaming with pride.

"So sergeant, is that how the enlisted men do it?" he asked.

The sergeant replied, "Well, sir, usually they just ride it into town..."

FAMILY SECRET

Dear Abby,

I have a problem. I have two brothers. One of them is a boatswains' mate in the Navy, and the other was put to death in the electric chair for a gruesome multiple murder. My mother died from insanity caused by syphilis when I was three years old. My three sisters are prostitutes, and my father is a child molester who sells narcotics to high school students.

Not long ago I met a girl who was just released from prison. She was sentenced for smothering her illegitimate child to death, and I want to marry her.

My problem is this - if I do marry this girl, should I tell her about my brother in the Navy?

Signed,

In a Dilemma

SUPERIOR FIREPOWER

Back in the 1970's, during the Carter years, military budgets were slashed drastically and the armed forces were hard pressed for equipment.

During that time a soldier enlisted in the army. On the first day of training the troops in his unit were lining up to get their weapons, and this fellow was near the end of the line. When they got to him the armorer said they didn't have any more rifles, so they gave him a broom instead and told him to point it at people and say, "Bangitty, bangitty, bang!" So he thought, "Oh great, I come here to fight for my country, and they give me a stupid broom."

The next day they were lining up for bayonets, and he was at the back of the line again. When they got to him, again he was told they didn't have any left, so they gave the soldier a carrot and told him to tie it to the end of his broom, stab people with it, and say, "'Stabitty, stabitty, stab." He thought to himself, "Yeah great, I'm gonna go out there and get myself killed. Just what I always wanted."

Eventually the unit was sent to combat, and as the soldier walked out onto the battlefield he decided he'd at least try it out, rather than just stand there and be killed. He went up to someone, pointed the broomstick and said, "Bangitty, bangitty, bang!" and the guy fell over dead... so he thought, "My God! This actually works!"

He then went up to another person, thrust the carrot forward and said, "Stabitty, stabitty, stab," and again the guy died. So he went around killing people with his broomstick and his carrot, thinking, "Wow! This is so cool!"

Then he saw a guy standing all by himself, and the soldier thought, "Easy target. I'm going to go get him." So he went over and said, "Bangitty, bangitty, bang," and nothing happened. He went closer and did it again, and still nothing happened. So the soldier thought, "Oh no! It must be out of bullets! But how do you reload a broom?" So he went even closer and said, "'Stabbity, stabbity, stab. Stabity stabbity stab!" Still nothing happened.

Then, as the soldier was standing there trying to figure out what the problem was, the guy he was trying to kill ran over him, and as he did so he was saying, "Tankitty, tankitty, tank..."

NO PAIN, NO GAIN

It was a normal training day at the Navy SEAL training base in Coronado. The whole unit was lined up in formation, and the Chief Petty Officer in charge was walking around inspecting his men. There were rows of sailors stacked behind one another waiting to be inspected. The Chief got to the first squad leader, stood in front of him and punched him in the stomach the hard as he could. After about a minute, the squad leader caught his breath. The Chief then bellowed, "Did that hurt sailor?"

The sailor said, "No, sir!"

The Chief shouted, "Why not?"

Then the sailor replied, "Because I am a Navy SEAL!"

The Chief then got to the second squad leader, stood in front of him, and kicked him in the kneecap. After about a minute, when the sailor was finally standing again, the Chief hollered, "Did that hurt?"

The sailor responded, "No, sir!"

And the Chief said, "Why not?"

The sailor shouted back, "Because I am a Navy SEAL!"

The Chief then moved on to the third squad leader, and noticed that there was an erection between his legs. The Chief picked up a stick, and whacked the erection with it as hard as he could. The man doesn't make a sound... so the Chief asked him, "Did that hurt, sailor?"

And the sailor said, "No, sir!"

The Chief then asked, "And why not?"

The sailor pointed at the man standing behind him and said, "Because it was *his!*"

HUNTING DOG

In the Blue Ridge Mountains there was a retired sailor who was reputed to have the best hunting dog ever. He went by the name of "Chief."

One day three Marine Corps generals went up into the mountains and wanted to rent him. The old sailor said, "He's a good hunting dog... gonna cost ya fifty dollars a day." The generals agreed, and three days later they came back with the limit.

The next year the generals came back, and "Chief" had gotten even better. "Gonna cost you *seventy-five* dollars a day this time," he said, and again the generals agreed. Two days later, they came back with the limit once again.

The third year the generals came back and told the old sailor they had to have "Chief," even if it cost a *hundred* dollars a day. The old sailor replied, "You can have the worthless mutt for *five* dollars a day, and I'm overcharging you by four!!"

The bewildered Marines asked, "But we don't understand. What happened to him?"

"Well, a crew from the Navy base in Norfolk came up and rented him. One of those idiots called him *Master* Chief, and ever since then he's just been sitting on his lazy ass barkin'..."

VETERAN'S BAR

Four retired veterans were walking down the street, and when they saw a sign that said "Veterans' Bar" they decided to go in and have a drink. The bartender asked for their order, and they all ordered a martini. He delivered the drinks and said, "That will be forty cents."

They couldn't believe their good luck! The vets finished the drinks and ordered another round, and the bartender again said, "That will be forty cents." At this point their curiosity got the better of them, so

206

they asked the bartender, "How can you afford to serve martinis for a dime apiece?"

The bartender replied, "I guess you've seen the decor here. I'm a retired Sergeant Major, and I've always wanted to own a bar. Last year I hit the lottery for forty-five million, and decided to open this place for real veterans. Every drink costs a dime - wine, liquor, beer. It's all the same."

Right about then the vets noticed four guys sitting at the other end of the bar who hadn't ordered anything.

They asked, "So... what's with them?"

The bartender rolled his eyes and said, "Oh, those are retired Navy Chiefs... they're waiting for happy hour!"

MILITARY DISCOUNT

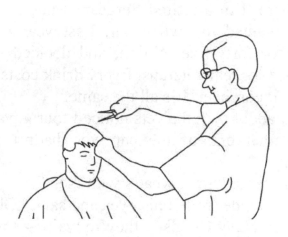

In a small town near Washington, D.C. a barber opened his shop for business, and a young enlisted Marine came in to get a "high and tight."

The barber asked the Marine about his service, and a lot of small talk ensued. After the haircut was complete the Marine opened his wallet to pay, and the barber said, "It's on the house, Marine. Thanks for your service to this great nation."

The next morning as the barber went to open his shop, there was a box on his doorstep. In the box was a note of thanks from the Marine and a bright red SEMPER FI T-shirt. That same morning a young airman came in for a haircut, and the same thing happened. They talked about the Air Force and made other small talk, and after the haircut was complete the airman stood and reached for his wallet.

The barber once again said, "No thanks, son. It's on the house. Thank you for your service to our country."

The next morning, as the man is opened his barbershop, on the doorstep was a box containing an Air Force ball cap and a thank you note.

That same day, a Navy captain came in for a haircut decked out in his full dress blues. The barber was impressed - and again, the same thing happened, small talk about the service. When the Captain tried to pay the barber once again said, "Not required sir, it's on the house. Thanks for your service to this great nation."

The next morning, as the barber went to open his shop, there on his doorstep… were three more Navy captains!

THE LAST WORD

A Marine and a sailor were sitting in a bar one day arguing over which was the superior service.

After a swig of beer the Marine said, "Well, we had Iwo Jima."

Arching his eyebrows, the sailor replied, "We had the Battle of Midway."

"Not entirely true," responded the Marine. "Some of those pilots were Marines. In fact, Henderson

Field on Guadalcanal was named after a Marine pilot killed at the Battle of Midway."

The sailor responded, "Point taken."

The Marine then said, "We Marines were born at Tun Tavern!"

The sailor, nodding agreement, said, "But we had John Paul Jones."

The argument continued, on and on, until the sailor came up with something he thought would end the discussion once and for all. With a flourish of finality he said, "The Navy invented sex!"

The Marine took a long pull from his beer, smiled, and replied, "That may be true, but it was the Marines who introduced it to women!"

"OFFICIAL" CORRESPONDENCE

"The Army just authorized ALL soldiers to wear the black beret. Stop laughing. No, really, it's right here in the message..."- Sometimes truth is stranger than fiction!

To Err Is Human, To Forgive Divine

To Err Is Human, To Forgive Divine

*****UNCLASSIFIED*****
PRIORITY
00924
FTTUZYUW RUE ACM 05727 0411854-UUUU-
RUCRNAA RUWJCFA
ZNR UUUUU RUCLRFA
P 11103Z FEB 82
FM CMC WASHINGTO DC
TO ALMAR
ACCT NA-CNRF GENERAL MESSAGE (37)
BT ACTION = G1 (5)
UNCLASS //N05803// SECTION 01 OF 01 SSEC (3)
ALMAR 036/82 ALL (1)
CMC MMOA-3/OA OA-I(2) CP-2(2)

SUBJ: PROCESSING OF UNMARRIED WOMEN
MARINES

1. DUE TO THE ENORMOUS EXPENSES ASSOCIATED
WITH MAINTAINING AN EFFICIENT RECRUITING
SYSTEM AND THE ADDITIONAL EXPENSE AND
INCONVENIENCE OF DISCHARGING UNMARRIED
WOMEN MARINES WHO ARE UNABLE TO
COMPLETE THEIR ENLISTMENTS DUE TO
UNAUTHORIZED PREGNANCY THE FOLLOWING
DIRECTIVES HAVE BEEN EFFECTED:

(A) UPON CERTIFICATION BY THE MEDICAL
DEPARTMENT THAT THE SUSPECTED FEMALE
MEMBER HAS REACHED THE STATE OF IMPENDING
MOTHERHOOD, SHE WILL BE TRANSFERRED TO
THE PRENATAL BATTALION, U. S. NAVAL BASE,
BAIMBRIDGE, MARYLAND FOR DUTY: SUCH DUTY

TO BE IN A TAD STATUS AND TO BE TERMINATED UPON THE BIRTH OF THE CHILD.

(B) THE CHILD WILL BE REGISTERED WITH THE LAST NAME OF THE SUSPECTED OR LIKELY FATHER AND A SERIAL NUMBER ASSIGNED. AS TO ANY CASE WHERE EXTREME DOUBT AS TO WHO THE FATHER IS, THE NAME OF THE SENIOR ENLISTED MAN AT THE LAST DUTY STATION OF THE MOTHER AT THE TIME OF CONCEPTION, WILL BE ASSIGNED.

(C) THE CHILD WILL BE MAINTAINED AT THE NAVAL NURSERY UNTIL THE AGE OF EIGHT (8) YEARS AT WHICH TIME IT WILL BE TRANSFERRED TO THE NAVAL ORPHANS FACILITY TO BE MAINTAINED UNTIL THE AGE OF EIGHTEEN (18), WHEREUPON IT WILL BE ENLISTED IN THE MARINE CORPS AND THE MILITARY OCCUPATION OF THE PARENT OF HIS/HER SEX WILL BE ASSIGNED. IF THE CHILD IS FATHERED BY A CIVILIAN OR NAVY SEABEE THE CHILD WILL BE PLACED AND ASSIGNED DUTY IN A U. S. ARMY INFANTRY BATTALION. CHILDREN OF THIS CATEGORY ARE EXPECTED TO POSSESS AN EXTREMELY LOW GCT.

(D) AT THE CHILD'S TIME OF ENLISTMENT THE PARENT OF THE SAME SEX WILL BE NOTIFIED AND IF HAVING COMPLETED TWENTY (20) YEARS OF SERVICE, BE PERMITTED TO RETIRE. UNDER THIS SYSTEM, IT IS EXPECTED THAT THE MARINE CORPS WILL REPRODUCE ITSELF AT A SUFFICIENT RATE TO PERMIT THE PHASE OUT OF THE MARINE

CORPS RECRUITING PROGRAM ENTIRELY. ALSO, IT
MAY BE NECESSARY TO CURTAIL THIS PROGRAM
IN THE FUTURE, AS ESTIMATED TURNOVER OF
PERSONNEL IS EXCEEDED.
BT

DEPARTMENT OF THE NAVY
HEADQUARTERS UNITED STATES MARINE CORPS
WASHINGTON, D. C. 20380

mmcp/mm/DRD
MCBul 1040
25 May 1983
MARINE CORPS BULLETIN 1040

From: Commandant of the Marine Corps
To: All Marines

Subj: Early Retirement Program

1. Information.

As a result of automation as well as the declining need of combat situations, and lack of wars, the Commandant must, out of necessity, take steps to reduce our forces. A reduction plan has been developed which appears the most equitable under the circumstances. Under this plan - older Marines will be placed under early retirement thus permitting the retention of Marines who are representative of the Marine Corps.

2. Scope.

a. A program to phase out the older personnel by the end of the current fiscal year via early retirement will be placed into effect immediately, this program shall be known as RAPE (Retire Aged Personnel Early).

b. Marines who are RAPED will be given an opportunity to seek other jobs within the Marine Corps, provided that while they are RAPED, they request a review of their past performance before actual retirement takes place. This phase of the operation is called SCREW (Survey of Capabilities of Retire Early Workers).

c. All Marines who have been RAPED or SCREWED may also apply for a final review. This is called SHAFT (Study by Higher Authority Following Termination).

3. Action. Program policy dictates that Marines may be RAPED once and SCREWED twice, but may get the SHAFT as many times as the Marine Corps deems appropriate.

M. MacMoose
By direction

To Err Is Human, To Forgive Divine

UNITED STATES MARINE CORPS
Marine Corps Base
Camp Pendleton, California 92055

BO 5216.18
BK:rjb:edh
24 Oct 1982

From: Commanding General
To: Distribution List

Subj: SOP for Death, Cessation of Life, and Dying

1. Purpose. To set forth and reaffirm Marine Corps policy in regard to unauthorized dying by enlisted personnel and junior officers who do so with complete disregard for the proper procedures pertaining thereto.

2. Background.

a. It has been brought to the attention of this Headquarters that personnel described in paragraph 1, above, are dying without proper authority or consent of their superior officers. In addition to being definitely unauthorized, this heinous practice is detrimental to the efficient operation of the United States Marine Corps and the accomplishment of its assigned mission. Consequently it must be discontinued immediately.

b. The manpower shortage is still acute in this theater of operations and any person who dies, without first obtaining permission through proper channel (via the Chain of Command), commits a serious offense and will be the subject of appropriate disciplinary action under the existing provisions of the Uniform Code of Military Justice.

3. Action.

a. Under no circumstances will an enlisted man or junior officer be permitted to die on government time. The following movements for Death, Cessation Life, and Dying shall be considered Standard Operational Procedure, to be utilized during off-duty hours only:

(1) On the receipt of the command "Die" victim will die in cadence by the numbers as follows:

(a) The victim will stagger a full 30 inch step, followed by a full 20 inch step, at the same time causing the eyelids to come to half mast and the eyes assume a fixed position.

(b) The victim will then sink slowly (in a military manner) to the knees, counting cadence silently, fall on the face with arms outstretched and thumbs at a 45 degree angle to the arms.

(c) The toes will be drawn together sharply, heels together, feet at a 45 degree angle.

(d) The last breath will be taken as follows:

((1)) Inhale two (2) metric liters of oxygen

((2)) Make one (1) low moan followed by a sharp gasp.

NOTE: The "Death Rattle" will not be used except for parades, reviews, and/or ceremonies; and, then only when authorized by a General Officer.

(2) Before dying, a map (F. Form 3212, presently not in stock) of the most recent route to Heaven will be drawn from the nearest S-3 Office, clearly marked with the victim's name, rank, serial number and EDoD (expected date of death).

(3) The route of travel will be strictly adhered to. Any detour for the purposes of liquid refreshment will be punishable by lengthy confinement in the subterranean chambers at the parent command. Depending upon the destination of the victim, rations will be drawn from the nearest S-4, to include:

Cake, Angel Food (not an item of standard issue), or
Cake, Devil's Food (presently in short supply).

(4) No victim will make the trip twice. All personnel opting for the scenic route will draw travel pay at the following rate:

Officers: $1.75 per mile
Enlisted: $ .05 per mile

(5) Advance per diem is authorized. It is recommended that you draw not more than 75% of the estimated cost of the per diem as an advance to preclude the possibility of an overpayment and subsequent reimbursement to the government. Under current regulations, advance per diem will not normally be paid more than 10 days prior to the date specified as the EDoD. While en route, use of government

quarters and messing facilities is directed. If not available, retain all receipts pertaining to the cost of quarters and messing.

b. Upon arrival at destination, victim will report to the Pearly Gates Transient Area Number 2 for administrative processing, angelification and sanctification or, in some cases, reassignment. Depending upon classification and assignment, the following equipment will be drawn:

(1) Upper strata personnel
WINGS, M1A1, pair, folding, white
HARP, M6A7, six string, gold or anodized brass
CLOUD, M01A/B, white, fleecy/cumulus reversible
HALO, M1957A2, round, lighter than air, gold or anodized brass

(2) Subterranean strata personnel
HORNS, X01A2, pointed, forehead mount
TAIL, X01A2, pointed, scaly, w/barb
FORK, M3A3, pitch, three tine, case hardened, w/sharpening file

c. Equipment will be shined, dusted, and lightly oiled where appropriated. A weekly PM will be held. Clouds will be inspected daily for excessive condensation. Halo will be worn one inch above the right eyebrow. Horns will be worn one on each upper corner of forehead. Pitchforks will be carried at Port Arms until arrival at the lower level.

d. All personnel will be governed by Military law while awaiting reassignment. Personnel scheduled for subterranean levels will be placed in an involuntary confinement status until their time of departure for their new duty assignment.

4. Reserve Applicability. The provisions of this Order are applicable to Fleet Marine Corps Reserve personnel aboard this base that are on active duty for training, extended active duty for training or fleet assistance program.

P. T. BARNUM
Chief of Staff

ABOUT THE AUTHOR

Officer candidates begin Crucible training

CPSIA information can be obtained
at www.ICGtesting.com
Printed in the USA
BVHW071127170620
581539BV00005B/304